# EMBROIDERY PROJECTS BOOK

# EMBROIDERY PROJECTS BOOK

Consultant Editor: Jane Iles

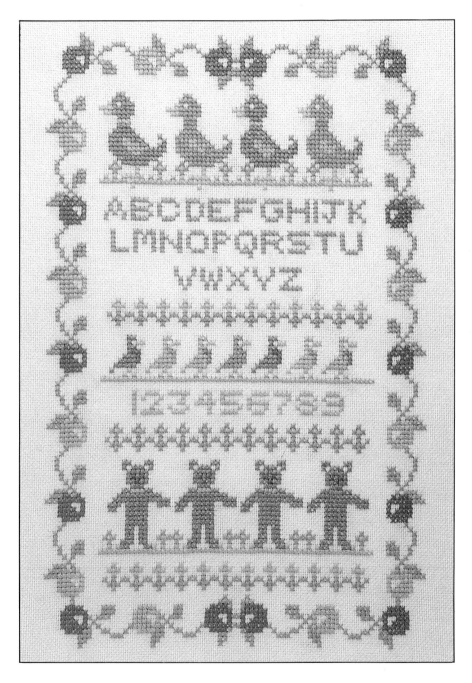

COLLINS

First published in this hardback edition in 1990 by
William Collins Sons & Co. Ltd
London · Glasgow · Sydney
Auckland · Johannesburg · Toronto

© This edition William Collins Sons & Co. Ltd 1990

Consultant editor: Jane Iles
Copy editor: Barbara Dixon
Designers: Michael Leaman and TL Creative Services
Illustrations by Tracey Davis, Terry Evans, Hannah Hammond,
Margaret Leaman, Jill Shipley
Index: Susan Bosanko

This material first appeared in: *Learn Crafts* series published by Collins, © all
photographs and illustrations William Collins Sons & Co. Ltd 1985, 1986, 1987, 1990
(*Learn Ribboncraft*, © text William Collins Sons & Co. Ltd 1985; *Learn Patchwork*,
© text/project design Lynette-Merlin Syme 1986; *Learn Lacecraft*, © text/project
design Audrey Vincente Dean 1986; *Learn Embroidery*, © text/project design
Jane Iles 1987; *Learn to Make Home Furnishings*, © text/project design
Jane Newdick 1987); *Superstitch* © Eaglemoss Publications Limited 1989.

Original series editor: Eve Harlow

A CIP catalogue record for this book is available
from the British Library.

ISBN 0 00 412594 0

Typeset by Nene Phototypesetters Ltd
Colour reproduction by Dot Gradations,
South Woodham Ferrers, Essex
Printed by Cronion, Barcelona, Spain

# Contents

# Introduction

The art of embellishing fabric with decorative stitchery has been practised throughout the world for centuries. Distinctive techniques and designs have evolved and been handed down lovingly from generation to generation so that today we can benefit from an enormous wealth of stitches, styles and methods.

One of the greatest attractions that embroidery has to offer is that it can be practised at almost any age and with the minimum of tools and materials. Indeed, some of the brilliantly coloured peasant embroideries found throughout the world have been worked by children with only the crudest needles and threads. Today, however, at the other end of the spectrum there is a steadily growing area of embroidery which relies heavily upon the facilities offered by hi-tech machines, man-made fibres and yarns, and synthetic dyes.

The *Embroidery Projects Book* introduces you to the world of embroidery and textiles by encouraging you to begin with some easy stitches and simple skills, and then progress to more advanced techniques. Even if you have never used a sewing needle before, you can learn many of the techniques of embroidery with the help of this book and also become familiar with some of its related crafts like patchwork and appliqué. With a little practice and patience, you will soon be able to brighten up many household items, as well as personalising clothing and producing that extra-special hand-made gift.

Within each chapter there is a host of delightful embroidery projects that encourage you to learn and get to know the basic stitches such as straight stitch, back stitch, and cross stitch, and then to use them in conjunction with techniques such as enlarging a design, following a chart and using fabric dye crayons.

The projects vary in size and complexity, and there is a wealth of ideas for you to work from. Some projects are quick to make and use only the cheapest materials, such as the Peruvian-style Cushions (page 16) which are made from dishcloths; others require a carefully chosen selection of good quality fabrics which are beautifully worked together,

uch as the Friendship Quilt (page 120). You
re shown how ribbons can be used instead
f threads to produce a pretty floral design
nd a charming townscape, while modern
nachine-made lace is used luxuriously on
illows and cushions, shawls and veils.

Step-by-step diagrams are included for all
he stitches in the book, as well as how-to
nstructions on stitches and seams for making
p the projects. You will soon be tempted to
xperiment and incorporate some of the

embroidery stitches you have seen in the early
chapters with other techniques such as
patchwork and appliqué.

Embroidery offers an amazing range of
creative work and rewarding results – from
colourful modern simplicity to traditional
charm and elegance, and with practice and
new-found confidence, the full breadth of the
world of embroidery will quickly become
apparent to you.

# Chapter One

# Making a Start

One of the biggest setbacks when one is thinking of taking up a new craft is the equipment that has to be bought. Almost any craft is costly at the beginning. This is not so with embroidery. All you really need to start this absorbing, satisfying and rewarding occupation is a piece of fabric, a needle, some thread or yarn and a pair of scissors.

## Materials and equipment

If you sew, you will probably find that you have most of the equipment you need in your sewing box.

### Fabrics
The fabrics you need to begin embroidery are all around you in your home – dishcloths, handkerchiefs, dish-towels, bed linen, towels, clothing and scraps of dressmaking fabrics, for instance. You do not need to buy expensive embroidery fabrics at the outset. Use what you have around you until the time comes when you want to work a special project. You can also experiment with different materials – ribbons, plastic canvas, lace and beads, for example.

### Needles
Ordinary sewing needles are not always suitable for embroidery work, as the eyes are too small for most threads

other than sewing cotton.

Two kinds of embroidery needle are mostly used: tapestry needles and crewel needles. Tapestry needles have large eyes and blunt, rounded tips and are used for working tapisserie yarn and thick threads through linen-type and heavy weave fabrics (as well as canvas). Crewel needles are finer and have pointed tips and large eyes. The patterns in this book usually recommend the needle size required for the thread. If you are ever in doubt as to the size of needle you should be using, remember that the thread should slip into the needle eye easily, and the needle should pass through the fabric easily.

A selection of different-sized ordinary sewing needles is always useful so that you can choose the most suitable to use when working a patchwork project for instance or making up many of the other projects.

### Threads
When you are working a project, it is

advisable to buy the type of thread recommended. In this book you will read about stranded embroidery cotton, Coton à Broder, Coton Perlé or Pearl cotton, soft embroidery cotton, crewel wool, tapisserie wool, basting and sewing threads, all-purpose polyester thread, and machine embroidery thread.

When you are practising stitches, use thread or yarn which you happen to have at hand – even knitting wool. Later, you will be interested to try the different types of yarns and threads available.

**Stranded embroidery cotton** This comes in a skein and is a smooth, slightly lustrous thread comprised of six loosely twisted strands. The strands are easy to separate (see Fig 6, page 10) and can be used singly or in combinations.

**Pearl cotton or Coton Perlé** This is a twisted thread with a rich, silky appearance and comes in balls as well as skeins. It comes in three thicknesses: No 8 is very fine, No 5 is slightly thicker, and No 3 is the thickest.

**Soft embroidery cotton** This is the thickest of all embroidery threads and is similar to crochet or knitting cotton. It is dull, with no sheen.

**Coton à Broder** This is similar to Coton Perlé, has a shiny finish and is a finely woven thread, usually used for detailed work.

**Crewel wool** This is a fine, two-ply twisted yarn, popular for embroidery.

**Tapisserie wool** This is thicker than crewel wool and is primarily used for canvas work where stitches cover the background canvas.

**Basting and sewing threads** These are used for general sewing purposes while making up many of the projects. Basting threads may be inexpensive white cotton threads used to temporarily hold layers of fabric together or mark a design and are later removed. You can also use leftover threads from other sewing projects. A collection of different coloured sewing threads is always useful for sewing small items such as attaching a ribbon bow or lace motif to a cushion.

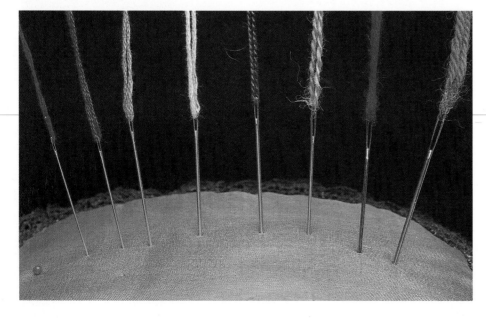

**All-purpose polyester thread** This is a very popular man-made thread which as its name suggests is suitable for use in many projects where both machine and hand sewing are involved.

## Machine embroidery thread

Special cotton thread in a large range of colours is sold for machine embroidery, but ordinary cotton machine thread is perfectly suitable. Do bear in mind the size of your project when choosing thread as machine thread is more economical than ordinary thread and you may be surprised by the amount of thread that is used in machine embroidery.

## Scissors

For embroidery, you will eventually need to buy a short pair of scissors, about 12.5cm *(5in)* long, with pointed tips. Only use them for embroidery cutting because, if they are used to cut anything like paper, the blades will become blunt and virtually useless for cutting fine fabrics and threads.

### Machine embroidery

Any sewing machine can be used for decorative stitching but, of course, the more basic the machine the smaller the range of patterns which are possible. If your machine has a special embroidery stitch feature you will be able to create a wide range of pictorial and abstract designs.

# Transferring designs to fabric

There are different ways of transferring designs to fabric and most of them are featured in this book.

**Direct tracing onto fabric** If the embroidery fabric is thin enough for the lines to be seen through it, place the fabric over the design and trace off the lines. Use a coloured crayon as this will wash out in laundering without spoiling the fabric.

**Fabric transfer pencils** These are sold in various colours and it is a very good idea to have several colours by you because, if you trace off pattern areas in a colour which is near to the thread colour, there is less likelihood of the lines showing under the stitchery. The most common type is used to draw the design on tracing paper. The paper is then placed face down on fabric and, with the heat of an iron, the design is transferred.

**Dressmaker's carbon paper** This is liked by some embroiderers but others find that it tends to smudge on the fabric. Place the carbon paper face downwards on the fabric, with the design tracing on top. Draw firmly over the pattern lines with a sharp tool.

**Templates** These are usually made of card and are made by tracing off the pattern outline and then transferring it onto card. The shape is cut out and then placed on the fabric and drawn around.

**Tracing paper and basting** This is a time-consuming method but it is often useful when working with thick, rough fabrics. Lay the traced design over the fabric and pin. With basting thread in a contrasting colour to the fabric, work small basting stitches all over the design lines. When completed, gently tear away the paper, leaving the basting threads on the fabric as a guide to embroidery.

**Tracing patterns** The phrase 'trace the pattern' will appear in several projects in this book. You will need tracing paper, which can be purchased in sheets or in pads from stationers or art shops, or, alternatively, you could use kitchen greaseproof paper. You may find it necessary to hold the book page to the window, with the tracing paper lightly taped over it, to make the tracing.

**Photographic enlargements** It is a good idea to enlarge complicated patterns

# Graph patterns

Many magazines and pattern books feature graph patterns, and there are several in this book. You may want to enlarge a pattern for a particular use, and this is done by making a graph pattern.

The apple motif from page 48 is used as an example.

Trace the motif and then draw a box round it. Divide the box into squares (Fig 1).

Fig 2 shows how the square is enlarged to the size required. Draw a diagonal line through and draw the new, larger box.

Divide the new box into the same number of squares as Fig 1.

From Fig 1, copy the apple onto the new grid by marking in small crosses or dots where the design lines touch the background grid lines.

Join the marks with a line so that the apple is reproduced larger (Fig 3).

You can use the same procedure to reduce the size of a design.

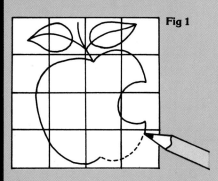

**Fig 1** *Enlarging graph patterns: trace the motif and draw a box round. Divide the box into squares*

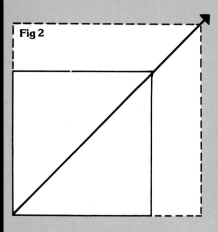

**Fig 2** *Draw a square the same size as the box and draw a diagonal line. Draw box to new size*

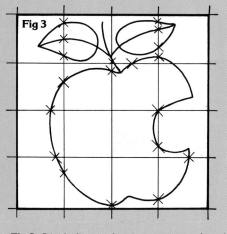

**Fig 3** *Divide the new box into same number of squares as Fig 1. Copy motif onto the grid*

photographically. Many quick-print shops now have photostat machines which will enlarge an image to the size required.

## Preparing fabric for embroidery

You will often be recommended to work from the centre of a design outwards to the edges. Also, many commercial pattern charts indicate the middle of a design with arrows set at the sides. You therefore need to mark the middle of your fabric before starting embroidery.

When working with a very fine fabric, measure the width and depth of the fabric with a tape measure. Mark the middle of both long sides and both short sides with pins and then work lines of basting threads between the pins. Where they cross is the middle of the fabric (Fig 4).

When you are working with an evenweave fabric (see Evenweave fabric, page 11), count the threads along one long side and along one short side to locate the centres. Work

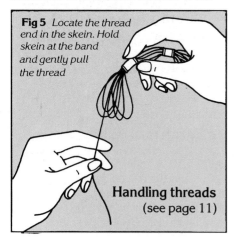

**Fig 5** *Locate the thread end in the skein. Hold skein at the band and gently pull the thread*

**Handling threads**
(see page 11)

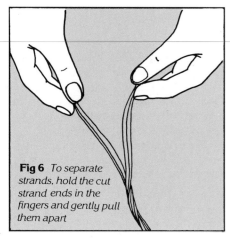

**Fig 6** *To separate strands, hold the cut strand ends in the fingers and gently pull them apart*

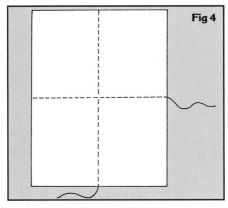

**Fig 4** *Marking fabric: work basting stitches horizontally and vertically to find the middle*

basting threads across and then down the fabric, starting at these points. The middle is where the threads cross.

### Frames and hoops

You will not need an embroidery frame or

hoop when you first start embroidery because most of the earlier projects in this book can be worked freely in the hand. However, you will almost certainly want one later.

A circular frame, consisting of two hoops, is used for small pieces of embroidery or on those occasions when the work would be distorted if it were not supported by a frame.

A square or rectangular frame can be made and this will be of great value to you. Use 2 × 2cm *(³⁄₄ × ³⁄₄in)* whitewood and cut accurately measured lengths with mitred corners. Fix these together with nails and PVC adhesive. If you prefer you can make a frame where two long sides butt up to two short sides. To use the frame, stretch the fabric over it and fasten with drawing pins or staples. An old picture

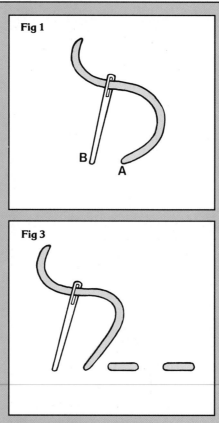

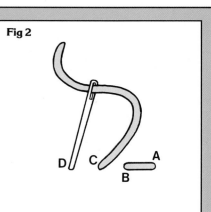

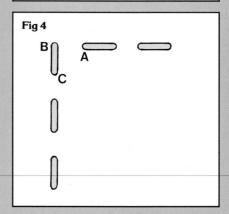

## Running stitch

1. Tie a small knot on the thread end. Bring the needle through from the wrong side at A and insert the needle at B, a short distance away (Fig 1).
2. Bring the needle out at C and insert it at D. Two stitches have now been worked (Fig 2).
3. Continue in the same way (Fig 3).

Running stitches should all be of the same length but the spaces between the stitches can vary, as long as you are constant in spacing throughout the piece of work.

**Turning corners**
Having reached the corner (Fig 4), bring the needle out at A and insert it at B, then bring the needle out at C, and a square corner is made.

frame can also be used for a frame, or a stretcher, purchased from an art shop, will do very well.

# Handling threads

When you get your new skeins of thread you will see that they are formed so that a strand is loose at one end. Hold the skein as shown in Fig 5 and pull the end. You will find that the thread pulls out easily without tangling.

To separate one or two strands, cut the thread from the skein and hold it as shown in Fig 6 and gently pull the threads apart.

## Starting and finishing thread

Although in some cases, it is acceptable to tie a knot in the thread end, you should try not to get into the habit of always doing this because it will spoil the look of your embroidery on the wrong side.

To make a neat start, push the needle through the fabric about 5cm (2in) from where you will begin stitching, leaving a 'tail' on the right side. Then bring the needle through at the point you intend to begin stitching. When this thread end is finished, take the thread to the wrong side and darn the end into embroidery already worked.

Then thread the 'tail' into the needle, take this through, and darn in the end.

When cutting thread, never cut more than 45cm (18in). This is about the most you can comfortably handle.

When working motifs, it is best to finish off the thread end and start again on the next motif. It looks untidy when stitches are taken across the back of the work.

**Top left:** *Pattern darning stitches (see page 12) worked decoratively, with thread ends left in a fringe.*
**Above:** *Pattern darning and Straight stitches worked together.*

# Evenweave fabric

When fabric is woven, the vertical threads (called the warp) are held on the loom. The weft threads are woven through the warp threads. Most fabrics used for embroidery are in a plain weave where the weft goes alternately over and under the warp threads (see diagram). When both the warp and weft threads are of the same weight the fabric is called evenweave fabric and you will find references to this in different projects in this book. Evenweave fabric is used for counted thread stitches (such as Cross stitch) where fabric threads are counted with the needle tip to position the stitch correctly and to ensure that stitches are of the correct size.

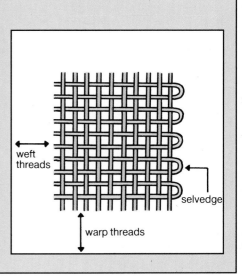

weft threads

selvedge

warp threads

# The first stitch

The first stitch in embroidery is a small, straight stitch called Running stitch. The needle and thread pass into the fabric and then come out a distance away, and then continue, passing in and out of the fabric, leaving stitches on the fabric surface (see Figs 1 and 2, page 10).

Running stitch can be quite small, covering only two or three threads of fabric – or it can be longer, from 6mm–12mm (¼–½in) long. It is a very simple stitch to do but, worked in bright threads and with the stitches varying in length, it can be very decorative.

You can use patterns of Running stitches to decorate all kinds of items – children's and babies' clothes, lingerie and nightwear, jeans and jackets and, for the home, tablecloths, dishcloths, place mats, cushions and curtains. Running stitches worked through curtain net look very individual, worked in embroidery thread of the same colour or in a contrasting shade.

## Pattern darning

Pattern darning is a technique used in many parts of the world. It has been worked by embroiderers as a decoration for garments, robes and furnishings for more than 2000 years.

In principle, stitches are worked through an evenweave fabric to make patterns (see picture on page 11). They can be worked close together, so that the background fabric is entirely covered, or the fabric can be part of the colour scheme.

Stitches can be worked horizontally (like Running stitch), vertically, or they can slant diagonally.

To practice pattern darning, you will need a piece of openweave embroidery fabric called binca which has a defined square weave, making it easy to position stitches correctly. If this is not available, you can use a piece of hessian or sacking (burlap).

# Additional stitch library

Throughout the book you will find step-by-step illustrations showing you how to work the embroidery stitches used in the projects. Illustrated below are some additional stitches which will be of use.

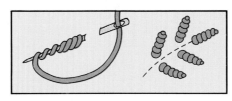

## Bullion knots

1. Bring the needle up at A. Take a fairly large stitch from B to A but do not pull the needle through. Twist the thread six or seven times round the needle.
2. Pull the needle through, easing the twisted thread close to the fabric with your thumb. Re-insert the needle at B.

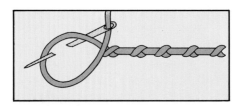

## Coral stitch

Bring the thread through to the front of the fabric. Working from right to left, lay the thread along the stitching line, securing with your thumb. Now make a tiny stitch across the stitching line, a little distance away, under the laid-down thread and over the loop of thread to catch it in a knot. Continue making stitches an equal distance apart. Make them close together or spaced out, as you wish.

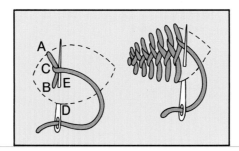

## Cretan stitch

This makes a very useful filling stitch because of its close, woven effect.

Work from left to right. Bring the needle through above the centre line of the design at A. Take it down at B, and bring it out at C, catching the thread under the needle.

Take the needle down at D, a little to the right of B, and bring it up at E, catching the thread under the needle. Make each stitch as even as possible.

## Feather stitch

Bring the thread through to the front of the fabric. Make a loose stitch by inserting the needle level with this point, and bring it up lower down, so that when the thread is looped under the needle, it makes a V. Pull the needle through. Make stitches to right and left alternately.

## Double Feather stitch

Make three stitches to the right, then make two to the left, two to the right, and so on. Slope the needle from right to left when working to the right, and vice versa.

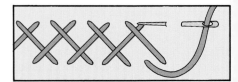

## Herringbone stitch

This is often worked between parallel lines, but may be used to fill a shape, as in the sampler. Bring the thread up on the bottom line and make a small running stitch along the opposite line, so that the thread lies diagonally across the fabric. Note that the stitch is worked from left to right, but the needle always points from right to left. Now make a small running stitch to the right of the first one, and along the bottom line. Continue, leaving a small space between running stitches.

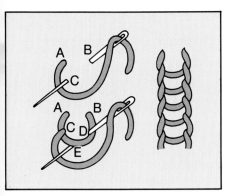

## Open Chain stitch

Bring the needle up at A, take it down at B, and bring it out at C, just below A.

Pull the thread through, but leave a wide loop. Take the needle down at D, inside the loop on the opposite side, then bring it out at E, forming the next loop in the chain.

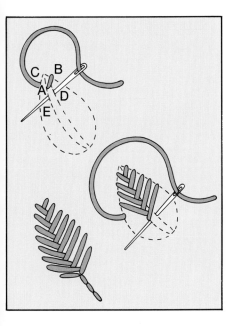

## Open Fishbone stitch

This is worked in the same way as Fishbone stitch except that the stitches are spaced evenly apart to give an open effect. The overlapping of each stitch is also more pronounced.

(To work plain Fishbone stitch, close up each stitch and overlap slightly less.)

To work the stitch, bring the needle up at A and insert it at B. Bring it up again at C, then make a sloping downward stitch to D. Make a small stitch to bring the needle up at E ready to repeat the process. Continue in this way, varying the length of the slanting stitches to accommodate your design.

## Picot loops

Picots are small decorative additions to Buttonhole stitch (see page 56) and overcast edges and bars. They are small loops (see A below), but can also be worked as tiny Bullion Picots or Buttonhole Ring Picots to give extra detail. The picots around the heart on page 99 are worked by adding the tiny loops evenly along a line of Running stitch (see B below), but could also be represented simply by weaving your thread loosely in and out of the mesh of the tulle where you wish a small loop to be positioned.

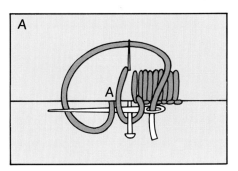

**Picots and Buttonhole stitch** Insert a pin, point upwards, where the picot is to be placed. Loop your thread under the pin and pass the needle through the fabric edge at A. Bring the needle up from under the fabric edge looping the thread and weaving the needle horizontally under the pinned loop and through the larger loop. Pull the thread until a tight knot is formed around the picot loop. Remove the pin ready to continue Buttonhole stitches.

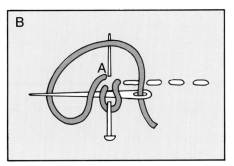

**Running stitch** is used here with picots. An additional tiny stitch is worked at A and then the needle and thread is looped and woven as for the picot and Buttonhole stitch.

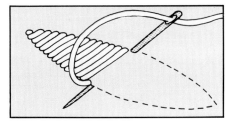

## Satin stitch

Make a series of straight stitches lying close to each other. Bring the needle up and re-insert it on the other side of the motif being worked; bring the needle up again very close to where it first went in, being careful not to pull the first stitch too tight. Continue across the motif in this way.

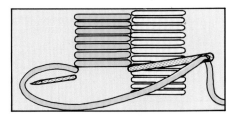

## Encroaching Satin stitch

When you need more than one row of satin stitch to cover an area, you can work the ends of the second row stitches between the ends of the stitches on the first row. The two rows will blend together smoothly. Encroaching satin stitch is often used for subtle tone variations in the shade of the thread.

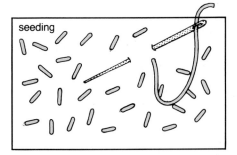

## Seeding

Make a series of tiny back stitches to fill an open area, placing them an even distance apart and at different angles, scattered over the fabric.

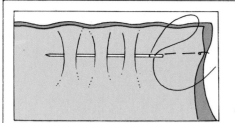

**Fig 1**  *Basting*

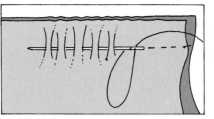

**Fig 2**  *Running stitch*

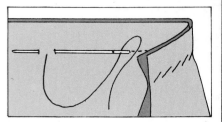

**Fig 3**  *Backstitch*

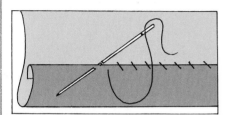

**Fig 4**  *Hemming*

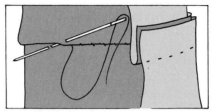

**Fig 5**  *Slipstitch*

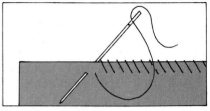

**Fig 6**  *Oversewing*

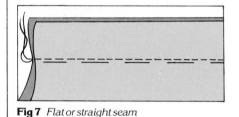

**Fig 7**  *Flat or straight seam*

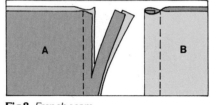

**Fig 8**  *French seam*

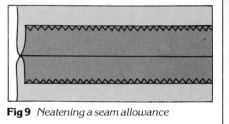

**Fig 9**  *Neatening a seam allowance*

# Stitches and seams for making up

Only a few stitches and seams are needed for making up the projects in this book.

## Basting

This is used to hold two pieces of fabric together temporarily and also provides a guide to help you to achieve a straight seam.

Begin with a double Backstitch. Pick up 6mm (¼in) stitches on the needle spacing them 6mm (¼in) apart.

## Running stitch

Running stitch has many uses in sewing (see page 12). In Fig 2 it has been used for gathering.

Begin with a double Backstitch. Pick up several tiny stitches on the needle, all of the same length, with the same amount of fabric between stitches.

## Backstitch

Backstitch can be used for working seams. Properly worked, it looks very like machine-stitching.

Begin with a double Backstitch, then

bring the needle through from the back about 3mm (⅛in) forward along the seam line.

Re-insert the needle about 3mm (⅛in) behind the point where the thread came through and bring it out again 3mm (⅛in) forward on the seam line.

Continue inserting the needle at the end of the last stitch and bringing it through 3mm (⅛in) ahead.

## Hemming

Hemming is used to hold hems in place. This is usually worked with the work held over the forefinger. Take a tiny stitch, then bring the needle diagonally through the edge of the hem. Space stitches 6mm (¼in) apart.

## Slipstitch

This is used to join two folded edges invisibly on hems and for attaching trims.

Bring the needle through just under the folded edge of fabric. Slide the needle through the fold for about 6mm (¼in) then pick up a thread or two of the under fabric or adjacent fold.

## Oversewing

This is used on raw edges to prevent them fraying.

Work from right to left or left to right. Work diagonally-placed stitches over the raw edge, keeping them evenly spaced and all of the same length.

# Seams

## Flat or straight seam

This is the most commonly used seam. Secure the machine thread with a few reverse stitches, then stitch beside the basting line. At the end of the seam, work a few reverse stitches.

## French seam

This is used where raw edges are required to be enclosed for a neat finish or for a hard-wearing seam.

With wrong sides of fabric facing, stitch a seam 6mm (¼in) from the edge. Trim the seam allowance (Fig 8a).

Re-fold the fabric so that right sides of fabric are together and stitch along the seam line (Fig 8b).

## Neatening seam allowances

If the sewing machine has a zigzag stitch facility, work zigzag-stitching along the raw edges of the seam allowance after stitching the seam. Use oversewing if the neatening is to be done by hand.

# Fun and fashion

Children enjoy wearing decorations on their clothes – embroidered motifs on shirts, jeans, skirts and suits. Purchased character motifs are simple to apply and the techniques for doing this are on page 102.

Here are some motifs that can be used for appliqué or embroidery – or they can be painted with fabric paints directly on to the garment pieces. Trace the motifs, then transfer them to the fabric with dressmakers' carbon paper.

## Measurements

Throughout the book measurements are given in both metric and imperial. Whichever system you use it is important to follow it throughout the project you are working on as occasionally the conversions given are not the exact equivalent.

### Table of Conversions used in this Book

| cm | yds | m | yds |
|---|---|---|---|
| 20 | ¼ | 3.5 | 3⅞ |
| 35 | ⅜ | 3.6 | 4 |
| 50 | ½ | 3.75 | 4⅛ |
| 91 | 1 | 4 | 4½ |
| | | 4.5 | 5 |
| m | yds | 5 | 5½ |
| 1 | 1⅛ | 6 | 6⅝ |
| 1.1 | 1¼ | 7.5 | 8¼ |
| 1.2 | 1⅜ | 8.25 | 9 |
| 1.4 | 1½ | 12 | 13¼ |
| 1.45 | 1⅝ | 14 | 15⅜ |
| 1.6 | 1¾ | 16.5 | 18 |
| 1.85 | 2 | 33 | 36 |
| 2 | 2¼ | | |
| 2.15 | 2⅜ | cm | in |
| 2.3 | 2½ | 1 | ⅜ |
| 2.5 | 2¾ | 2 | ¾ |
| 2.6 | 2⅞ | 2.5 | 1 |
| 3 | 3¼ | 3 | 1¼ |

| cm | in | cm | in |
|---|---|---|---|
| 3.5 | 1⅜ | 31 | 12½ |
| 4 | 1½ | 33 | 13 |
| 4.5 | 1¾ | 34 | 13½ |
| 5 | 2 | 35 | 14 |
| 6 | 2¼ | 37 | 14½ |
| 6.5 | 2½ | 38 | 15 |
| 7 | 2¾ | 40 | 16 |
| 7.5 | 3 | 41.5 | 16¼ |
| 9 | 3½ | 42 | 16½ |
| 9.5 | 3¾ | 43 | 17 |
| 10 | 4 | 45 | 18 |
| 11.5 | 4½ | 50 | 20 |
| 12.5 | 5 | 53 | 21 |
| 14 | 5½ | 56 | 22 |
| 15 | 6 | 60 | 24 |
| 16 | 6½ | 63 | 25 |
| 18 | 7¼ | 66 | 26 |
| 19 | 7½ | 70 | 28 |
| 20 | 8 | 75 | 30 |
| 22 | 8½ | 80 | 31 |
| 23 | 9 | 81 | 32 |
| 24 | 9½ | 84 | 33 |
| 25 | 10 | | |
| 26 | 10¼ | mm | in |
| 27 | 10¾ | 1.5 | 1/16 |
| 28 | 11 | 3 | ⅛ |
| 28.5 | 11¼ | 6 | ¼ |
| 29 | 11½ | 12 | ½ |
| 30 | 12 | 23 | ⅞ |

# Straight Stitch

Straight stitch can be a counted thread stitch or a free-style stitch, depending on the fabric and the design. Both forms are in this chapter. You are shown how to work Peruvian-style cushions on dishcloth cotton, embroider a shirt with a 2000 year-old Arab pattern, work a set of place mats, create daisy-sprigged curtains and embroider a garden – all with Straight stitches.

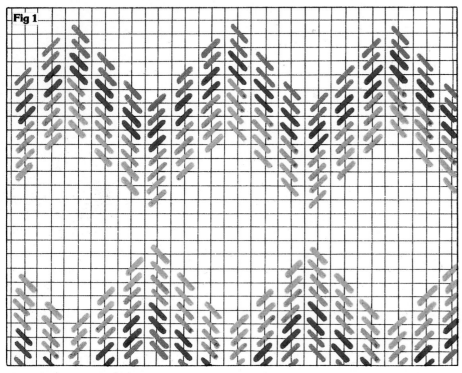

**Fig 1** *Pattern for the zigzag cushion with part of an adjoining zigzag. Follow the colour sequence*

**Fig 2** *One-quarter of the tasselled cushion pattern. The black arrows indicate the middle of the design*

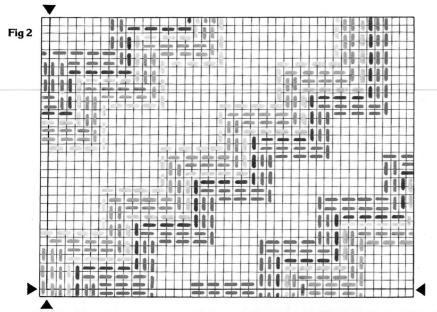

## Peruvian-style cushions

Soft cotton dishcloths with an open weave are used to make these bright cushions. Inspiration for the patterning is taken from the bold, geometric designs that have decorated Peruvian peasant clothes for hundreds of years.

### Materials required
*For both cushions*
4 cotton dishcloths with an open weave, approximately 33cm *(13in)* square
70cm *(28in)* of 91cm *(36in)*-wide cotton fabric
Double knitting yarns, 1 ball each of emerald green, jade green, royal blue, bright pink (for the zigzag cushion), plus bright red, turquoise and yellow (for the tasselled cushion)
Tapestry needle, size 18
White sewing thread
Two 30cm *(12in)*-square cushion pads

### Preparation
Cut four 33cm *(13in)* squares from the cotton fabric. Take two of the dishcloths and attach each of them to a cotton square, pinning round the edges. Baste all round and remove the pins. Machine-stitch all round, 6mm *(¼in)* from the edge. Remove the basting stitches.

### Working the embroidery
Work the embroidery on the two remaining dishcloths.

Fig 1 is the pattern for the zigzag cushion and shows a complete zigzag, with part of the adjoining zigzag. Repeat this pattern across the dishcloth following the colour sequence as shown in the picture (pink, royal blue, jade green, emerald green).

Fig 2 is one-quarter of the tasselled cushion pattern. The black arrows indicate the middle of the design. Fig 3 shows how the four quarters are worked to make up the whole pattern. Measure the dishcloth to find the middle and mark this with basting threads (see Fig 4, page 10 for the technique).

To work this project, you may tie a knot in the yarn end, although it is better to take a double stitch around the edge of the fabric to secure the end. Starting at the edge, pass the needle

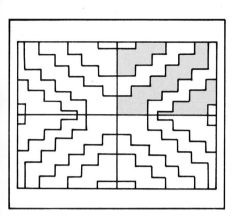

**Fig 3** *Repeat the pattern Fig 2 as shown to make the complete tasselled cushion*

smoothly through the fabric, working over and under threads as shown in the charts. Do not pull tightly on the stitches but ensure that they lie smoothly on the fabric surface. Work each line of the design with one length of yarn.

Leave the yarn ends hanging at the edges or finish them, without pulling up, with a double stitch through the fabric edge.

## Making the cushion

When the embroidery is completed, mount the dishcloth fabric on a piece of cotton fabric as you did for the cushion back. Place the front and back together, right sides facing, and pin and baste on three sides. Machine-stitch, taking a 12mm *(½in)* seam. Remove the basting threads and turn the cover to the right side. Insert the cushion pad and close the open seam with hand-sewing. Work both cushions in the same way.

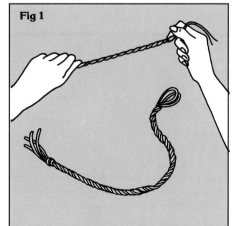

## Finishing

For the tasselled cushion, make sixteen tassels from the remaining yarn, following the instructions below. Sew four to each corner, as shown above.

For the zigzag cushion, cut 4m *(4½ yds)* of each of the remaining yarn colours and make a twisted cord, following the instructions given below. Apply the cord to the cushion edges as

follows: double the cord and form a loop. Sew the loop to one corner of the cushion. Continue sewing the cord to the four sides of the cushion, making and sewing loops on the two facing corners. On the last corner, tie the cord ends in a bow and sew to secure. Knot the cord ends about 10cm *(4in)* from the bow and trim to make tasselled ends.

# Twisted cords and tassels

**Cords** Cut wool yarn to 2½–3 times the finished length of cord required. Hold the ends firmly in each hand and twist the yarn. Continue twisting until the yarn coils upon itself. Allow the yarn to twist, then take the middle in one hand and the ends in the other and pull gently so that the cord straightens. Knot the ends together (Fig 1).

**Tassels** Cut several 10cm *(4in)* lengths of wool yarn. Fold in half to make a bunch. Tie a piece of yarn round the bunch as shown, knotting the ends. Trim the ends to the length desired (Fig 2).

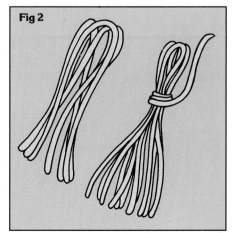

# Long stitch pictures

The technique of picture-making with long stitches originated in Scandinavia and it has become a popular type of needlework, especially for beginners and young people.

It is very easy to do and the work grows quickly so that the picture is soon finished.

The method is only suitable for pictures because the long threads lie on

## Straight stitch

Straight stitch can be worked vertically, horizontally or diagonally and the stitch length varies to fit the shape of the area being worked. Stitches are worked close together so that the fabric background is covered and does not show between the stitches.

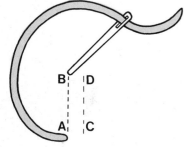

**Fig 1** *Vertically: work the stitch in the same way, bringing the thread through at A and inserting it at B. Bring the needle through at C and insert it at D to make the second stitch*

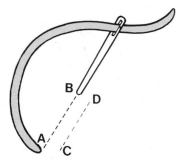

**Fig 2** *Diagonal stitches are worked in the same way. When working freestyle, make sure all stitches lie at the same angle*

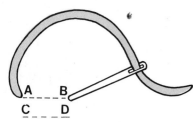

**Fig 3** *Horizontally: bring the needle through at A and insert the needle at B. To make the second stitch, bring the needle through at C and insert it at D*

the surface of the fabric and, if used for items such as cushions, the threads would catch in wear.

Two pictures are given here for you to work and practise the stitch. The tree picture is the simplest, with the background fabric forming part of the design. The country landscape is more difficult, with small areas to work.

## Tall tree

### Materials required
27 × 23cm *(10¾ × 9in)* piece of Aida fabric with 14 threads to 2.5cm *(1in)*
DMC Tapisserie wool as follows:
1 skein each of 7314 blue, 7771 bright green, 7364 mid-green, 7367 dark green, 7541 bottle green, 7402 light green, 7337 grey-green, 7619 brown, small amount of white
Tapestry needle, size 22

### Preparation
Trace the design from the picture and transfer it to the fabric using an embroidery transfer pencil.

### Working the design
Follow the picture for the direction of the stitches and colours. All the stitches are long stitches, set either horizontally or vertically. The only exception is the pair of birds which are worked with two diagonal Straight stitches.

## Country landscape

### Materials required
25 × 30cm *(10 × 12in)* piece of Hardanger fabric with 9 threads to 1cm *(22 threads to 1in)*
Paterna Persian yarn as follows: 1 skein each of 553 ice blue, 555 pale ice blue, 261 cream, 522 teal blue, 713

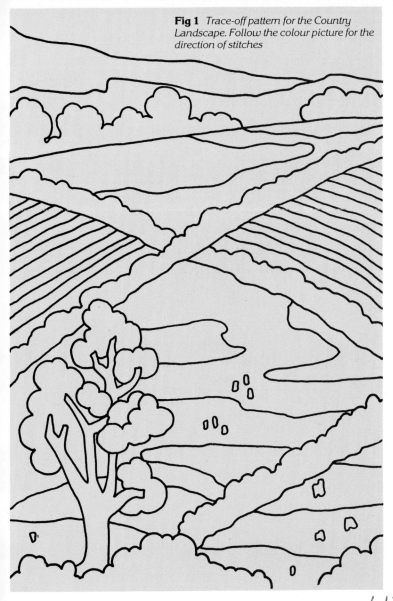

**Fig 1** *Trace-off pattern for the Country Landscape. Follow the colour picture for the direction of stitches*

mustard, 614 pale hunter green, 664 pale pine green, 612 mid-hunter green, 433 mid-chocolate brown, 403 mid-fawn brown, 405 pale fawn brown, 406 beige
Fabric transfer pencil and tracing paper (or dressmaker's carbon paper)
Tapestry needle, size 22

## Preparation
Trace the pattern (Fig 1). Trace over the lines on the wrong side of the paper with the fabric transfer pencil. Following the manufacturer's instructions, transfer the picture to the fabric. (If dressmaker's carbon paper is being used, follow the technique described on page 9.)

## Working the design
An embroidery hoop will make the work easier and will also help to prevent the yarn being pulled too tightly. If neither a hoop nor an old frame is available then great care must be taken to see that all the stitches lie smoothly on the fabric

without puckering.
Follow the picture for the direction of the long stitches. Note, for instance, that the ploughed fields have stitches lying diagonally (see illustration and the picture).

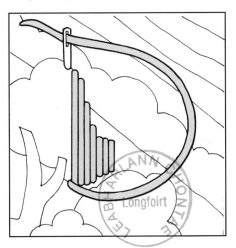

**Fig 2** *Here vertical Straight stitches are worked to different lengths, close together, to fill the design area*

## Finishing both pictures
When the embroidery is completed, cut a piece of stiff card and lace the picture as described on page 35. Alternatively, tape the fabric edges to the back of the card with adhesive tape.

**Fig 3** *Work Straight stitches diagonally for the ploughed fields, vertically for the grass, hedges and foliage with tree branches in horizontal stitches*

# Arab shirt

The shirt in the picture is made of cream evenweave fabric embroidered with a motif of triangles on the neckline and round the sleeves. The design was taken from an old Middle Eastern robe embroidery and Arab women have been working similar patterns on their garments for more than 2000 years.

Stitches based on Straight stitches are used mostly in Middle Eastern embroideries and brilliantly colourful designs are achieved.

## Materials required

*To work 1 neckline motif and 2 sleeve borders*
DMC stranded embroidery cotton as
   follows: 2 skeins each of 919 brown,

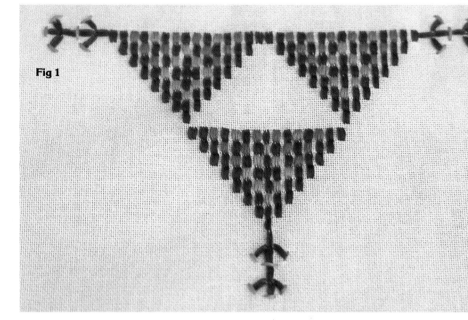

**Fig 1**

# Straight stitch on evenweave fabric

On evenweave fabric, fabric threads are counted to position the stitches correctly.
1.  Bring the needle through at A and insert it 6 threads above at B. Then, bring the needle through at C (1 thread to the left of A) and insert it at D, 6 threads

above and to the left of B. Work the third stitch of the block in the same way (E–F).
2.  To work the next block, take the needle 3 threads to the left and bring it out at G ready to make G–H, the first stitch of the next block.

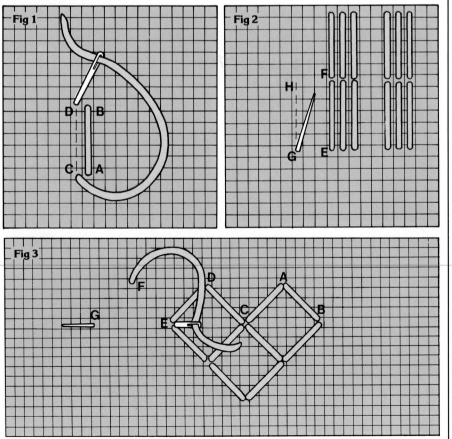

**Fig 1** *Detail of the Arab shirt neckline showing the arrangement of the Straight stitch pattern. Each stitch is worked vertically over 6 threads of fabric and there are 3 stitches to a block. Leave 3 threads between each block*

892 coral, 807 blue, 972 yellow, 905 green, 976 tan
Tapestry needle, size 24

## Working the design

Measure and mark the middle of the fabric (refer to Fig 4, page 10 for the technique).

The colour picture (Fig 1) above is a detail of the neckline motif and you can work the embroidery from this, matching thread colours and remembering that stitches are worked vertically over 6 threads of fabric in blocks of 3 stitches, set 3 threads apart.

Fig 2 is a section of the sleeve border. The blocks each have 2 stitches in them, worked over 6 threads of fabric and set 3 threads apart. The border has bands of Square stitch and working instructions for this are given in Fig 3.

**Fig 3** *Square stitch: The stitch is worked in two stages. In the first stage, the needle is brought through at A, inserted at B 4 threads down and 4 to the right, and brought out at C, 8 threads to the left and level with B. Insert the needle in the same place as A and bring it out at D, 8 threads to the left and level with A. Insert the needle at C again and bring it out at E, 8 threads to the left and level with C. Insert the needle at D again and bring it out at F. Insert at E and bring out at G and so on. This makes a series of half squares. Work the other half of the squares in the same way, reversing the stitch*

**Fig 2** *Section of the sleeve border pattern. Here, blocks have 2 Straight stitches in them, worked over 6 threads of fabric and 3 threads apart. Work Square stitch above and below the Straight stitch pattern (see Fig 3)*

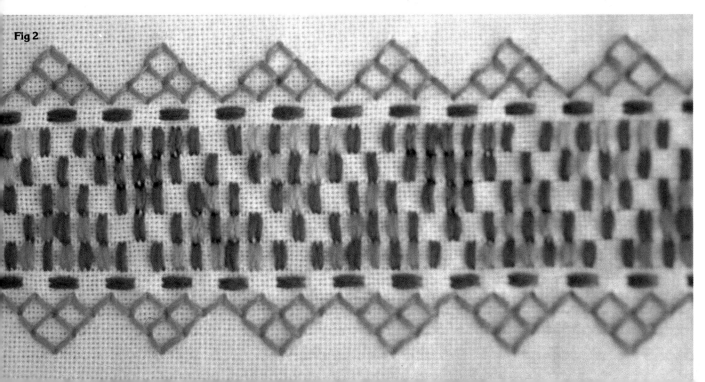

Fig 2

# Daisy-print curtains

Straight stitches can also be worked on finely-woven fabrics, such as the polyester lawn used for the curtains in the picture. Here, straight stitches are worked so that they radiate from a central point and the finished effect is like a daisy.

Daisies can be worked to any size and can have just eight petals as shown or have a number of petals close together. The embroidered daisies are worked over painted spots of fabric paint (see Fig 4).

## Materials required

White polyester lawn fabric, sufficient to make two curtains
Fabric paints in red, white, blue and yellow (or fabric crayons in pastel colours)
Paintbrush, items for printing 'blocks' (corks, bottles, bottle caps, etc)
Stranded embroidery threads in pink, pale blue and yellow
Crewel needle, size 7
White sewing thread

## Preparation

Wash, dry and iron the curtain fabric. Spread the fabric over clean newspaper and weight it at the corners so that it does not shift during printing.

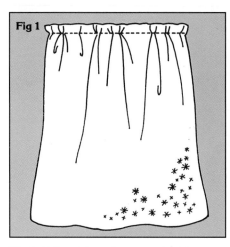

**Fig 1** *Follow this arrangement of daisies or work a random design of your own*

Mix the fabric paints according to the manufacturer's instructions.

Fig 1 shows the arrangement of the daisies on the curtain pictured. Follow this arrangement for your own curtains or work in a random fashion, printing colour spots to your own design.

Brush a little colour onto your chosen printing 'block' and press it firmly on the fabric. Spots can overlap if you like. Print all the spots and leave the fabric to dry. Print two matching curtains.

To fix the colour spots, spread clean cotton fabric over the printing and iron for 1–2 minutes with the iron at a very hot setting. Wash, dry and iron the printed curtains.

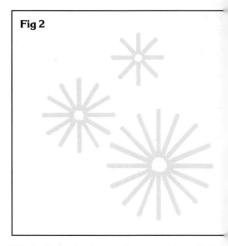

**Fig 2** *Trace the daisy patterns and transfer to the fabric using the direct tracing method*

## Transferring the pattern

Trace the daisies from Fig 2 and transfer them to the fabric, positioning daisies over the colour spots (see Fig 4). Any of the transferring methods described on page 9 can be used but the direct tracing method is recommended for this project.

## Working the design

The embroidery is worked with three strands of embroidery thread in the needle.

Divide a 38cm *(15in)* length as described on page 10.

Tie a single knot on the thread end. Work the daisies as shown in Fig 1 to

# Straight stitch daisies

In this project, Straight stitch is worked as a free-style stitch to form daisies. Stitches are worked over the transferred design lines.
1. Bring the needle through to the right

side of the middle of the daisy at A. Insert the needle at B (Fig 1).
2. Bring the needle through at A again and insert it at C (Fig 2).
3. Two petals of the daisy have now

been worked. Continue bringing the needle through at A and work each of the petals in turn (Fig 3). Finish the thread end on the wrong side at A with a tiny back stitch.

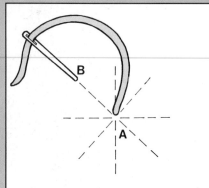

**Fig 1** *Bring the needle through to the right side at A and insert it at B*

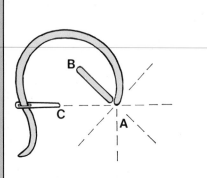

**Fig 2** *Bring the needle through at A again, ready to make the next stitch. Insert the needle at C to make the second petal*

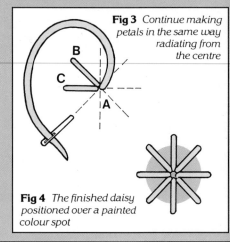

**Fig 3** *Continue making petals in the same way radiating from the centre*

**Fig 4** *The finished daisy positioned over a painted colour spot*

Fig 3, matching the thread colour to the printed circles. You may vary the length of the petals if you desire — it will help to give freedom to the finished embroidery.

Finish each daisy off as it is worked. Do not be tempted to work from one daisy to the next without finishing off the yarn because this will produce an untidy look on the wrong side — and both sides of a curtain show.

Work two matching curtains.

## Lining embroidered curtains
If you prefer to line your curtains, use the same white polyester fabric. Cut the lining to the same size as the curtain, then trim 4cm *(1¹/₂in)* from the long edges of the lining. Place the curtain and lining together, right sides facing, and pin and baste the long edges together. Machine-stitch.

Re-fold the curtain so that the lining is centrally positioned on the curtain. Press. Turn up the hem and machine-stitch. Finish the top edge with a casing or with curtain tape.

# Place mats

In this project, Straight stitches are worked close together to make Satin stitch. Cross stitches and Back stitches are also used in this design. The instructions for working these stitches are given on pages 30 and 45.

## Materials required
*For 2 place mats 40×28cm (16×11in)*
2 pieces of 50 × 38cm *(20 ×15in)*
evenweave embroidery fabric with 29
threads to 2.5cm *(1in)*
Anchor stranded embroidery cotton as
follows: 3 skeins of 850 marine blue;
2 skeins each of 311 tangerine, 361
light golden tan, 362 golden tan, and
848 light marine blue; 1 skein each of
313 tangerine, 889 brown
Tapestry needles, sizes 20 and 24

## Preparation
Mark the centre of both pieces of fabric
across the narrow width with basting
stitches (see Fig 4, page 10 for the

technique). Fig 1 is the chart for one
complete motif of the border design.
The background lines represent
threads of fabric and the heavier lines
represent stitches.

The open arrow is the centre of the
border and should coincide with the
line of basting thread. Fig 2 is the chart
for the corner motif. The key for stitches
and colours for both charts is given.

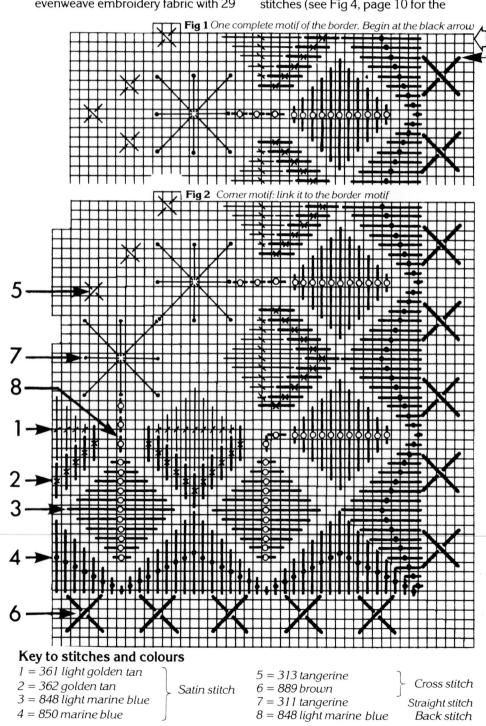

**Fig 1** *One complete motif of the border. Begin at the black arrow*

**Fig 2** *Corner motif: link it to the border motif*

## Key to stitches and colours

| | |
|---|---|
| 1 = 361 light golden tan | ⎤ |
| 2 = 362 golden tan | |  Satin stitch |
| 3 = 848 light marine blue | |
| 4 = 850 marine blue | ⎦ |

| | |
|---|---|
| 5 = 313 tangerine | ⎤ Cross stitch |
| 6 = 889 brown | ⎦ |
| 7 = 311 tangerine | *Straight stitch* |
| 8 = 848 light marine blue | *Back stitch* |

## Working the embroidery

Four strands of thread are used for the embroidery with the exception of those stitches worked in 850 marine blue, where six strands are used. Use the larger needle for this.

With the long side of fabric towards you and starting at the point marked with the black arrow on Fig 1, commence stitchery following the chart and the colour key. Begin the border 5cm *(2in)* from the edge of fabric.

Work the motif 9 times to the left and then work the corner motif (Fig 2). Turn the fabric and work the Fig 1 motif 11 times, then work the corner motif (Fig 2) and continue working Fig 1 motifs up to the basting lines. This completes half of the place mat. Complete the other half in the same way.

Make two matching place mats.

## Finishing

Press the embroidery on the wrong side. Trim the fabric to within 6cm *(2³⁄₈in)* of the embroidery, then turn a 2.5cm *(1in)* hem, mitring the corners (see page 114). Slipstitch the hem.

# Secret garden

The secret garden picture is in effect a painting done with threads. Long and Short and Straight stitches are worked at different angles, in grouped masses and individually, to catch the light and to interpret the foliage, grasses and flowers of a lush, overgrown garden.

The stitches completely cover the fabric and here you have the opportunity of adding some of your own ideas to the project when placing the stitches and choosing colour tones.

## Materials required

40 × 80cm *(16 × 32in)* piece of white cotton fabric

**Fig 1** *Trace-off pattern for the Secret Garden picture. The broken line is a guide for cutting the mount*

35 × 45cm *(14 × 18in)* piece of pale-coloured printed cotton fabric
Embroidery hoop 25cm *(10in)* diameter
Tracing paper
Felt-tipped pen
Anchor stranded embroidery cotton as follows: 1 skein each of 35 red, 316 orange, 375 soft brown, 347 brick, 117 pale violet blue, 158 very pale blue, 160 pale blue, 216 mid-sage, 225 emerald, 206 mid-forest green, 264 pale olive, 255 grass green
Crewel needle, size 7
28 × 38cm *(11 × 15in)* piece of strong card
23 × 33cm *(9 × 13in)* piece of strong card
Clear adhesive
Masking or adhesive tape

## Preparation

Fold the white cotton fabric in half and place it in the embroidery hoop, making sure the fabric is taut and evenly stretched.

From Fig 1, trace the outlines of the garden. Use a fine felt-tipped pen as this will dry and, unlike pencil, will not smudge on the fabric. Pin the traced design to the fabric and transfer the pattern using the basting thread technique (refer to page 10).

## Working the embroidery

Use three strands of embroidery thread throughout.

With this type of project, it does not matter where you begin and it is in fact preferable for you to be working several areas at the same time. Think of your embroidery as a painting, where it is better to work the whole subject rather than isolated shapes which will eventually fit together.

The stitches that are used are freely arranged and you do not have to count threads or make sure that they are identically placed. You are creating a garden and if, for example, you want to work some extra orange Cross stitches because you like the effect they create, then this is good. (Refer to page 30 for Cross stitch.) You are learning to recognise, select and reject design areas as well as to work new stitches.

The sky is worked in two shades of pale blue thread which is built up in Long and Short stitches (see Figs 1–5, page 28) which fit together and curve around the top of the design.

rounded bloom shapes. Work the branches in the darker brown thread building up the slightly jagged and angular shapes with lines of several single stitches.

The foliage around the edges of the garden is freely built up with several clumps of long Straight stitches using the three stronger shades of green so that they look like grassy plants.

## Working the flowers

Once you have worked all the foliage, you will have quite a large area of green. To break this up, you now add the flowers. The orange flowers are tiny Cross stitches worked randomly so that they look as if they are scattered over the tops of the grassy patches (refer to page 30).

The red and violet-coloured flowers are similarly worked to give this scattered effect but are made by grouping sets of two or three small stitches together, placing them in different directions as you did with the foliage of the trees.

Finally, the grassy patch is worked in the two pale shades of green with long Straight stitches placed horizontally across the garden to give the effect of shadows across a lawn. Work a few tiny clumps of brighter green stems and orange or violet flowers on the lawn to add interest to this smooth, flat area.

## Finishing

Once the embroidery is completed, remove the fabric from the hoop. If necessary, press it on the wrong side to remove any creases and to 'emboss' the depth of the stitchery on the right side.

Place the embroidery right side down on a clean, flat surface and centre the smaller piece of card on it. Stretch fabric over the edges of the card, pulling it with the fingers and working from the centres of opposite sides to give a smooth, tight effect on the right side of the embroidery. Cut across the corners to remove excess fabric which would be bulky when folded. Glue the turnings to the card with clear adhesive and then tape the fabric edges.

To make the fabric mount for the picture, use the arched dotted line on the pattern (Fig 1). Centre the original tracing on the larger piece of the card and cut out the shape with a sharp crafts knife.

With Straight stitches, work small clumps of grass randomly spaced over the printed cotton fabric to link it with the embroidery. As the clumps are well-

The trees are worked to give a completely different effect. The three stronger shades of green have been used in patches to give areas of dense leafy colour beyond the brick wall. The actual stitch construction is simple. Work clusters of about four closely grouped Straight stitches.

The clusters are then randomly scattered so that they are not facing the same way (see picture). This emphasizes the slight sheen of the stranded cotton as it picks up and reflects light. The larger patches of green can be 'lifted' by scattering a few isolated stitches of a different green on the leafy clusters or, alternatively, working some brown Straight stitches to represent the tree branches.

The wall is worked entirely in the brick colour 347, building up small oblong shapes with the stitches laying horizontally across the wall, leaving a small gap of bare fabric between each brick. Remember to stagger the positioning of the bricks from one row to the next and, as the wall becomes hidden by the garden foliage, you will have to fill in the small gaps where the bricks can still be seen with groups of smaller horizontal stitches.

The foliage of the large rose bush with the red blooms is worked in a similar way to that of the trees, but with a less dense effect, so that the wall can be seen between the leaves. The blooms are then built up with clusters of Straight stitches positioned to give the

spaced, each clump should be worked separately, starting and finishing off thread ends neatly so that there is no risk of the green thread showing through the fabric. Keep the tension even.

Press the fabric on the wrong side and place it right side down on a flat surface. Place the larger piece of card on it, centring it, and stretch the fabric onto the card. Cut out the centre section of the fabric, leaving 1cm (³⁄₈in) all round for turnings.

Clip into the curved upper edge and also into the lower corners so that the fabric can be smoothly stretched.

Fold the turnings onto the card, gluing it down and then taping the edges.

Finally, glue and tape the embroidered panel to the back of the window mount.

## Long and Short stitch

1. Bring the thread through at A and insert it at B (Fig 1). To make the next, longer stitch, bring the needle through at C and insert it at D, close beside B (Fig 2).
2. To make a short stitch, bring the needle through at E and insert it at F close beside D (Fig 3).
3. To work the second row, bring the needle through at G and insert it at H between 2 long stitches (Fig 4). The third row is worked as the second with stitches fitting into the second row (Fig 5).

# Greetings cards in stitchery

Greetings cards and 'thank you' cards, embroidered especially for the occasion, are always received with delight and they are fun to do. The cards in the pictures are all worked on a Christmas theme but every kind of occasion is an opportunity for working small, simple pieces of embroidery for cards.

Ready-made card mounts can be purchased from most needlework shops and are available in different sizes and styles. Mounts can also be made at home, using thin card or construction paper.

### Making card mounts

The size of the envelope will decide the dimensions of the card. Make the card about 3mm (¹⁄₈in) smaller all round so that it slips in to the envelope easily.

Round or oval-shaped windows are not recommended as these are difficult to cut cleanly.
1. Having decided the finished size of the card, draw the shape three times, edges touching, as shown in Fig 1. Measure and draw the 'window' on section 2. Using a sharp crafts knife, cut out the 'window'.
2. Using a large, blunt-tipped needle and a metal edged ruler, score along

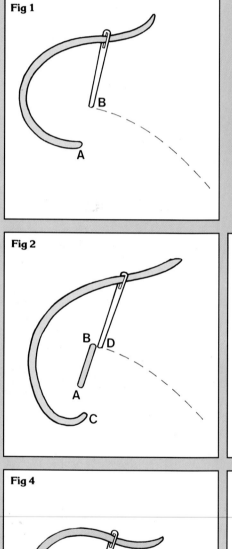

**Fig 1**

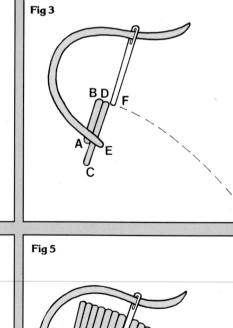

**Fig 4**

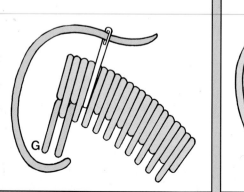

**Fig 5**

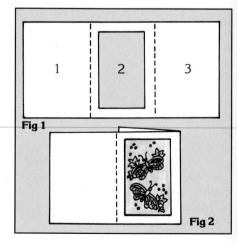

**Fig 1** *Draw the card shape three times, edges touching as shown. Cut a window in the centre section 2*

**Fig 2** *After mounting the embroidery on the wrong side of section 3, fold 3 onto 2*

the fold lines on the inside of the card. Fold on the scored lines.

3. Trim the finished embroidery so that it is a little smaller than the card. Spread a little clear adhesive, very thinly, on the edges of section 3, on the wrong side. Position the embroidery right side up and press on the edges to fix it in place. Leave to dry.

4. Spread a little clear adhesive, very thinly, round the window, keeping it at least 3mm (¹/₈in) from the edges. Press section 3 onto section 2. Fig 2.

### Motifs and designs

Motifs used for small cards should be simple and the effect will be more pleasing if stitches are kept to two or three kinds. Suitable motifs can be found in embroidery pattern books or you can trace designs from books, magazines, gift papers, etc. Some of the motifs given for Cross stitch on pages 32–3 are suitable for gift cards.

Patterns for the Christmas cards in the picture are not given but similar designs can be worked from the following details.

# Snowflake

*Size of motif, 5 × 5cm (2 × 2in)*
**Fabric** Blue evenweave linen, 28 threads to 2.5cm (1in).
**Threads** White stranded embroidery cotton, silver embroidery thread.
**Stitch** Cross stitch (page 30) over two threads of fabric.

# Sequin tree

*Size of motif, 6 × 4cm (2¹/₄ × 1¹/₂in)*
**Fabric** Finely woven dark green polyester/cotton.
**Threads and materials** Black stranded

embroidery cotton, silver embroidery thread, 26 gold sequins, 1 gold sequin star, 17 small green glass beads, 9 small red glass beads.
**Stitches** Straight stitch (page 18) and oversewing. To work the design, bring the needle through from the wrong side of fabric, pass it through a sequin, then thread on a bead and pass the needle back through the sequin. Proceed immediately to the next sequin without fastening off the thread.

# Candle glow

*Size of motif, 6.5 × 3cm (2¹/₂ × 1¹/₄in)*
**Fabric** Finely woven dark blue polyester/cotton.
**Threads** Stranded embroidery cotton in orange, peach and old gold, and silver

embroidery thread.
**Stitches** Outline the candle in silver thread with machine-stitching or by hand using Stem stitch (page 64). Work the flame in old gold in Stem stitch. Decorate the candle with rows of stitchery: Stem stitch, Chain stitch (page 50), Fly stitch (page 67) and couched Straight stitches (page 61).

Add groups of three French knots (page 61).

# Silver tree

*Size of motif, 9 × 4cm (3¹/₂ × 1¹/₂in)*
**Fabric** Finely woven dark green polyester/cotton.
**Threads and materials** Silver embroidery thread, pearlised sequins.
**Stitches** Work the tree shape with machine stitches or by hand using Stem stitch (page 64) or Back stitch (page 45). Sew on the sequins with silver thread. Work a small double Cross stitch (page 30) at the tree top.

# Three candles

*Size of motif, 4cm (1¹/₂in) square*
**Fabric** White evenweave embroidery linen, 24 threads to 2.5cm (1in).
**Threads** Stranded embroidery cotton in red, green and gold embroidery thread.
**Stitches** Use Cross stitch (page 30) for the candles, Straight stitch (page 18) for the candle flames and Fly stitch (page 67) for the tree branches.

# Chapter Three

# Cross Stitch

Cross stitch is popular with beginners because it is a very easy stitch to work and there are many designs available in pattern books which use it. In this chapter you are given a library of motifs so that you can make pretty accessories or design your own sampler. You will then feel ready to work a violet herb pillow, make bright Christmas decorations or stitch a 'Bear in bed' nightwear bag for a child.

## Small accessories

The accessories pictured are all decorated with Cross stitch and most of them can be worked in only a few hours. Some of the motifs are given as charts on pages 32–3.

**Framed baby name** Worked on Aida cloth with 11 holes to 2.5cm *(1in)*. Threads are DMC stranded embroidery cotton as follows: 776 pink, 334 blue, 913 green, 554 mauve, 445 yellow. (Chart for letters Fig 1.)

**Redcurrants** Worked on Aida linen with 14 holes to 2.5cm *(1in)*. Threads are DMC stranded embroidery cotton as follows: 349 red, 350 light red, 904 green, 907 light green, 221 brown-red. (Chart: Fig 2.)

**Key ring** Worked on Aida linen with 14 holes to 2.5cm *(1in)*. Threads are DMC stranded embroidery cotton as follows: 794 mid-blue, 956 bright pink, 957 mid-pink, 818 light pink, 745 yellow, 703 green, 310 black. Two strands used throughout. (Chart: Fig 3.)

**Duck picture** Worked on Aida linen with 14 holes to 2.5cm *(1in)*. Threads are DMC stranded embroidery cotton as follows: 973 yellow, 322 blue, 701 green, 666 red, white. To achieve the size, stitches are worked over 2 squares of the fabric. (Chart: Fig 4.)

**Porcelain box top** Worked on Aida linen with 14 holes to 2.5cm *(1in)*. Threads are DMC stranded embroidery cotton as follows: 793 blue, 794 light blue, 895 dark green, 3347 mid-green, 745 yellow, 335 dark pink, 963 light pink.

Two strands used throughout. (Chart: Fig 5.)

**Gardener's diary** Worked on Aida linen with 14 holes to 2.5cm *(1in)*. Threads are DMC stranded embroidery cotton as follows: 322 dark blue, 3325 light blue, 813 blue-grey, 318 grey, 922 orange, 402 light orange, 445 yellow, 890 dark green, 988 mid-green, 945 flesh. (Chart: Fig 6.)

**Hairband** Worked on embroidery riband 5cm *(2in)*–wide. Threads are DMC stranded embroidery cotton as follows: 890 dark green, 352 dark coral, 754 light coral, white. Work over two squares of the fabric. (Chart: Fig 7, border pattern.)

**Cushion** Worked on Aida linen with 14 holes to 2.5cm *(1in)*. Threads are DMC stranded embroidery cotton as follows: 798 blue, 957 mid-pink, 905 green. (Chart: Fig 8.)

**Cherries jam pot cover** Worked on Aida linen with 14 holes to 2.5cm *(1in)*. Threads are DMC stranded embroidery cotton as follows: 349 dark red, 352 light red, 350 medium red, 986 dark green, 988 mid-green, 472 light green. (Chart: Fig 9.)

**Paperweight** Worked on Aida linen with 14 holes to 2.5cm *(1in)*. Threads are DMC stranded embroidery cotton as follows: pink 893, mid-green 988, yellow 744. (Chart: Fig 10.)

**Pincushion** Worked on pink evenweave linen with 22 holes to 2.5cm *(1in)*. Threads are DMC stranded embroidery cotton as follows: 554 light mauve, 327 dark mauve, 550 purple, 445 yellow, 966 light green, 318 grey, 776 pink, 3350 dark pink. (Chart: Fig 11.)

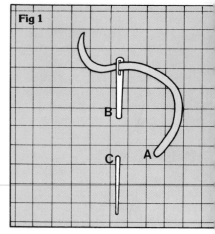

Fig 1

## Cross stitch

Cross stitch is a counted thread stitch and is worked on evenweave fabric. It can be worked from right to left or left to right, as you wish. The upper stitch of the cross can slant in either direction but it must lie in the same direction throughout a piece of embroidery.

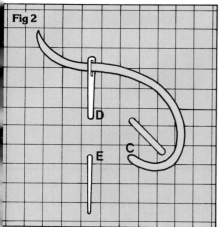

Fig 2

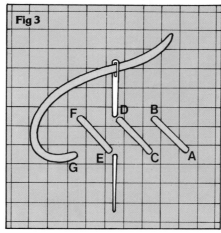

Fig 3

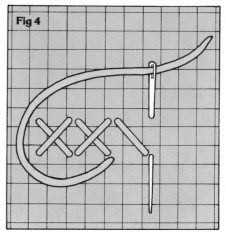

Fig 4

When working Cross stitch, it is a good idea to try always to go down through holes which have a stitch already in them and come up through empty holes.

1. Bring the needle through at A and insert it at B, two threads up and two threads to the left. Bring the needle through at C to complete half the Cross stitch (Fig 1).

2. From C, take the needle to D, two threads up and two threads to the left, then bring the needle through at E, to make half of the 2nd stitch (Fig 2).

3. Continue in the same way E–F.

To complete the cross, having brought the thread through at G, insert the needle at D (two threads up and two to the right), and bring it out at E (two threads down) Fig 3.

4. Continue in the same way completing the Cross stitches.

# Sampler motifs

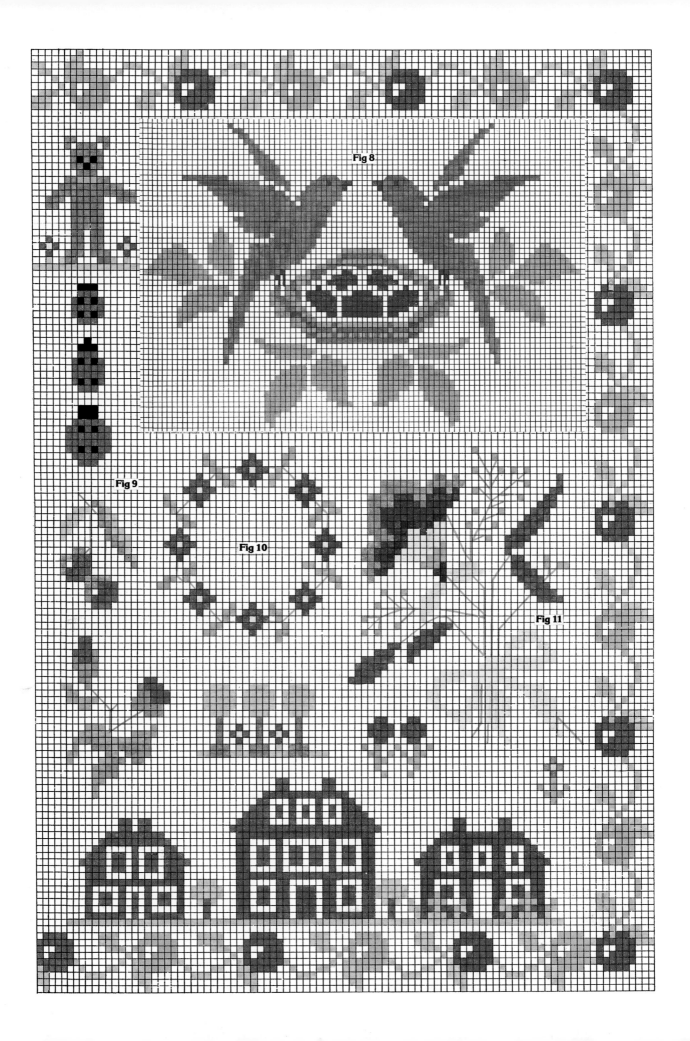

# First sampler

In the days before printed patterns, samplers were a means of recording embroidery designs and motifs and embroiderers would use them to try out stitches, colours and threads before using the designs in the final piece of work.

By the eighteenth century, samplers had become an accepted method of teaching young girls to do needlework and charming examples of their work can still be found today.

Although samplers are still popular as a form of needlework, few embroiderers bother to make their own designs nowadays, although it is by no means difficult to do. Samplers are an ideal way of recording family events and occasions – weddings, christenings, births, graduations and anniversaries – and, as such, make perfect gifts.

The sampler pictured is made up of children's motifs and an alphabet, and these motifs, with others, are given on pages 32–3. Using these motifs, you will be able to design your own sampler.

If a special motif you want is not given, it is possible to make your own from a picture or drawing from a book.

### Planning a sampler

Decide the overall dimensions first. You may, for instance, already have a frame you would like to use. Draw the area of the sampler on graph paper. Remember that every square represents one stitch and not a thread or hole.

Cross stitches can be worked over a single vertical and horizontal thread or over two or more threads. Count the number of squares on one long side and one short side of your chart and then count the number of stitches that will be worked on your fabric, to make sure that you have the size of sampler you require.

Select or design your motifs and plan any words or lettering. Copy these onto your graph paper chart, colouring them in the thread colours you intend using.

You may prefer to copy larger motifs onto pieces of graph paper and cut them out so that you can experiment with different arrangements.

When planning a border, start in the middle of the sides and work towards the corners. The design may have to be adjusted to go round the corners neatly.

### Preparing the fabric

Having made sure that your charted sampler is the size you want, count threads and outline the area for embroidery with basting threads. Count threads to find the middle vertically and horizontally and mark with basting threads (refer to page 10).

Cut out the fabric at least 10cm *(4in)* from the basted outline.

You may wish to mount the fabric in an embroidery frame for working, but you can also work the fabric freely in your hand.

### Using a Cross stitch chart

Count squares and mark the vertical and horizontal middle of the chart. It is a good idea to begin either with the lettering or the largest motif. Follow the basted lines and the marks on the chart to ensure that the embroidery is centred on the fabric.

You may find it helps to concentrate your eye on the motif you are working by cutting a hole in a piece of paper and pinning this over the motif, thus blocking out surrounding designs.

Have several needles threaded with

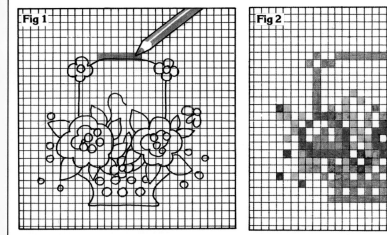

## Designing Cross stitch motifs

You will need some squared graph paper and coloured pencils or felt-tipped pens.

Trace the picture or drawing on tracing paper. Rub soft pencil over the back of the tracing and then draw over on the right side onto graph paper.

Each square of the graph paper is going to be a Cross stitch. Colour the squares following the traced outline. Sometimes the line will go through the middle of a square. This does not matter as long as the motif keeps its general shape. Choose the best squares to achieve the effect (Fig 1).

Fig 2 shows the basket motif coloured and ready for working the embroidery. The picture shows the basket worked in stranded embroidery cotton.

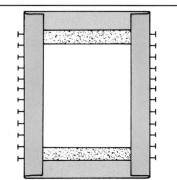

**Fig 1** *Fold and stretch fabric edges to the wrong side and insert pins to secure*

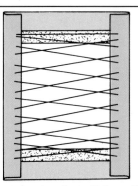

**Fig 2** *Lace edges together with long stitches as shown and then remove the pins*

**Fig 3** *Fold top and bottom edges to the wrong side, pin and lace the edges*

## Displaying and mounting embroidery

Embroidery must be mounted on card to display it properly, especially before framing. To do this, cut a piece of thick card to the desired size. If the fabric is thin and semi-transparent, it is a good idea to pad the card with a piece of non-woven interfacing. Cut it to the same size as the embroidery fabric.

Press the embroidery carefully on the wrong side and spread it right side down

on a flat surface. Lay the non-woven interfacing on top, matching edges. Lay the card on the fabric, centring it. Fold the two side edges onto the card, inserting dressmaker's pins into the edges as you work (Fig 1).

Thread a needle with a long length of thread and tie a small knot in one end. Pass the needle through the fabric at one end and work lacing stitches back and

fourth across the mount as shown in Fig 2.

While the lacing is being worked, continually stretch the fabric so that it is as smooth as possible. Remove the pins as you lace.

Fold in the other sides and pin, as before, and then work lacing to hold the fabric edges stretching the fabric smoothly (Fig 3).

Remove the pins.

different colours by you so that you can change colours quickly. When working a solid block of stitches the needle should, if possible, be brought to the front of the work through an unworked hole in the ground fabric, and go down through holes where stitches have already been worked. This will produce

a neat and even area of stitchery, as it prevents the possibility of previously worked stitches being split by the needle point.

Remember that it is important to work all the Cross stitches identically with the uppermost stitches facing the same way throughout.

### Finishing
When the embroidery is completed, carefully unpick the basting threads. The finished sampler should be lightly pressed on the wrong side, stretched and laced over a piece of thick card ready for framing.

**Fig 1** *Chart for the wild violet design. Match the colours here to the embroidery threads, following the key. Work each Cross stitch over 2 horizontal and 2 vertical threads*

### Violet pillow key

= M367 mid-green

= M989 light green

= M907 bright green

= M740 orange

= M743 yellow gold

= white

= M208 violet

= M554 pale violet

# Wild violet pillow

This Cross stitch project demonstrates how a small design or motif can be enlarged on graph paper to make a bigger design.

The wild violet design was adapted from a drawing on a small seed packet. The first stage was to trace the drawing and then transfer it onto a graph paper with very small squares. The outline was then copied onto paper with larger squares, thus enlarging the original drawing.

The chart was then coloured, copying the original seed packet colours. Each square of the chart represents 1 Cross stitch worked over 2 vertical and 2 horizontal threads.

If preferred, the original tracing could have been enlarged photographically and the graph paper chart made as described on page 35 (Figs 1 and 2).

## Materials required
*Finished size 35 × 28cm (14 × 11in)*
43 × 35cm *(17 × 14in)* piece of white evenweave fabric with 12 threads to 1cm *(27 threads to 1in)*
38 × 30cm *(15 × 12in)* piece of white fabric for backing the pillow
Madeira embroidery floss as follows: 1 skein each of M208 violet, M554 pale violet, M740 orange, M743 yellow gold, M989 light green, M367 mid-green, M907 bright green, white; 1 skein of Anchor Pearl cotton No. 5, colour 97 mauve (for edging cord)
Crewel needle, size 7
Coloured basting thread, sewing threads in white and mauve
Soft cushion pad

Sachet of lavender, pot pourrie or fragrant herbs (optional)

## Preparation
Press the fabric to remove any creases and mount it in an embroidery frame. (If you prefer, you can work the embroidery freely in your hand.)

Baste the horizontal and vertical centre guidelines, using coloured sewing thread (refer to Fig 4, page 10).

## Working the design
Three strands of embroidery floss are used throughout.

It is a good idea to begin working near the centre of the design to ensure that your embroidery is accurately placed on the fabric.

Following the chart (Fig 1), work the embroidery in Cross stitch (see page 30) working each cross over 2 vertical and 2 horizontal threads. Make sure that

all the stitches are worked with the uppermost stitch facing the same way throughout.

## Making the pillow
When the embroidery is completed, carefully unpick the basting threads. Press the fabric very lightly on the wrong side.
1. With the embroidered area centred, trim away the excess fabric to 38 × 30cm *(15 × 12in)*. With right sides together, place the pillow front and back together. Pin, baste and machine-stitch on two short sides and one long side, taking a 15mm *(⅝in)* seam.
2. Trim the corner points diagonally and turn the pillow to the right side. Push out the corners with a blunt pencil.
3. Place the cushion pad inside the embroidered case and turn in the raw edges of the opening. Hand-sew the edges to close.

## Finishing

Using the mauve Pearl cotton, make a twisted cord to go all round the pillow plus 30cm *(12in)* (see Fig 1, page 17). Sew the cord to the pillow using matching sewing thread, sewing on the seam line. Begin and end at the bottom right-hand corner. Tie the cord ends into a bow. To neaten the ends, tie a knot near to each end and then carefully fray out the loose threads to give a tasselled effect. If you prefer, make tassells as shown in Fig 2, page 17.

## Making a herb pillow

This kind of pillow makes a charming accessory if a sachet of fragrant herbs or lavender is put into the cushion pad.

Carefully unpick part of a seam and push the sachet into the middle of the pad. Close the seam with hand-sewing.

# Symbol charts

Some artist's materials shops and draughtsmen's suppliers stock sheets of clear acetate printed with squared grids of different sizes. These are extremely useful for making counted thread embroidery charts.

Simply place the grid over the drawing or photograph you wish to interpret into stitches. Copy the design onto squared paper.

Draw the design in chart form on the tracing paper, using symbols to represent the various colours.

Here is a simple symbol/colour guide you may like to use. This covers only twelve colours but you can invent other symbols for more colours.

| | | | |
|---|---|---|---|
| ⊡ | red | ◪ | brown |
| ▣ | blue | ■ | black |
| ⊠ | green | ◨ | pink |
| ▼ | yellow | ◣ | cream |
| ⫿⫿ | orange | ⊟ | crimson |
| ☐ | white | ✳ | navy blue |

# Christmas snowflakes

Soft, embroidered ornaments for the Christmas tree are very popular in Scandinavian countries and it is an idea worth copying. The small snowflake ornaments in the picture are made on binca fabric and take only a few hours to work.

The design given has two variations. In the first, the snowflake is simply worked in white Cross stitches on red fabric and then outlined with Back stitches using green thread.

In the second variation, an embroidery technique called Assisi work is used. In this, the motif is left unworked while the surrounding fabric is filled with Cross stitches. Traditionally, the design is then outlined with Back stitches, which can also be used for additional detail on the motif.

Assisi embroidery is said to have been evolved by the nuns in the Convent of St Francis in Assisi, Umbria, in central Italy. Local records show that, as early as the fourteenth century AD, this type of Cross stitch embroidery was being worked in designs abstracted from wood carvings.

## Materials required

*For each decoration, finished size 7cm (2³/₄in) square*

2 pieces each 9cm *(3¹/₂in)*-square of red binca fabric

Contrasting basting thread

Anchor Pearl cotton as follows: 1 skein each 01 white, 225 green (only part used)

Tapestry needle, size 24

Red sewing thread

38cm *(15in)* piece of 3mm *(¹/₈in)*-wide green ribbon (optional)

## Preparation

Count the holes along two sides of one fabric square to find the middle and mark the fabric with lines of basting threads vertically and horizontally.

## Working the embroidery

The middle of the design (Fig 1) is indicated with black arrows on the edges. This corresponds with the middle of your fabric, marked with basting threads.

Begin the embroidery in the middle of the design and work outwards.

After the Cross stitches have been completed, work green Back stitches (see page 45) around the snowflake, setting stitches the space of 1 Cross stitch away (Fig 2).

# Assisi snowflake

Prepare the fabric in the same way and work from the middle of the design (Fig

Green Back stitches can then be worked on the inside edge of the Cross-stitched background.

## Making up the ornament

Carefully remove basting threads. Place the embroidered square to an unworked square, right sides out and pin. Fold the ribbon as shown in Fig 4 and tuck it between the fabric squares at one corner. Baste to hold the ribbon in place.

Using red sewing thread, machine-stitch around the four sides of the ornament, stitching along the line of holes just outside the embroidery. Fray the threads away up to the line of stitching. Trim to a neat fringe (see picture). Remove basting threads.

If preferred, thread loops could be sewn to one corner of the ornament.

## Two-sided ornaments

If preferred, the ornaments could be embroidered on both sides – one side worked in the first way and the other in the Assisi variation. Other colour schemes could also be worked: green and red threads on white binca, or white and gold threads on blue binca, for example.

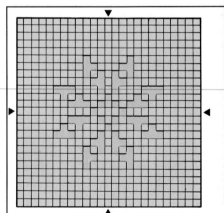

**Fig 1** *Work the design in white thread on coloured fabric or in coloured thread on white fabric. Each square represents one Cross stitch*

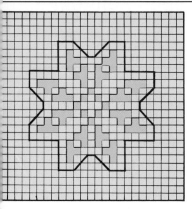

**Fig 2** *Outline the finished motif with green Back stitches (see page 45), setting stitches the space of 1 Cross stitch away*

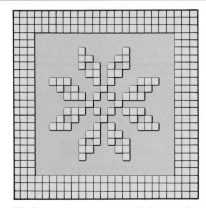

**Fig 3** *To work Assisi snowflakes, work the background to the motif in Cross stitches, leaving the motif as unworked fabric. Outline the motif with Back stitches if you prefer*

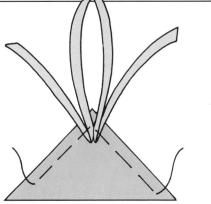

**Fig 4** *To make the ribbon hanger, fold the ribbon in half then bring the ends up as shown. Sew the hanger loop between fabric layers at one corner*

# Bear in bed

This nightwear bag is made of binca – a type of evenweave fabric with holes which enables stitches to be worked easily and accurately. Binca is an ideal fabric for practising Cross stitch because it has a square weave.

The bag has a drawstring top and is large enough to take a child's long nightgown or a pair of pyjamas. It would also make a shoe bag.

## Materials required

*Finished size 43 × 31cm (17 × 12½in)*
2 pieces each 50 × 35cm *(20 × 14in)* of white binca fabric
Anchor soft embroidery cotton as follows: 1 skein each of 290 yellow, 132 mid-blue, 229 emerald green, 238 light green, 335 bright red, 403 black, 352 brown; 2 skeins of 129 pale blue
Tapestry needle, size 24
Basting thread
White sewing thread
1m *(1⅛yd)* of white piping cord

## Preparation

On one piece of fabric, count the holes along one long side and one short side to find the middle of each. Work basting threads across and down the fabric. The middle of the fabric where the basting threads cross corresponds with the middle of the Cross stitch chart (Fig 1), indicated by the black arrows.

This embroidery can be worked freely in the hand or the fabric can be mounted in a frame.

## Working the design

Working from the chart and following the colour key, work the design in Cross stitch (see page 30). Start in the middle and work outwards to the border, making sure that the top stitch of each cross faces in the same direction.

## Making the bag

Press any creases from the fabric. Place the embroidered front and the bag back together, right sides facing. Pin and baste on the long sides and along the bottom.

Starting 3cm *(1¼in)* from the top edge, machine-stitch all round, taking a 15mm *(⅝in)* seam. Remove the basting threads.

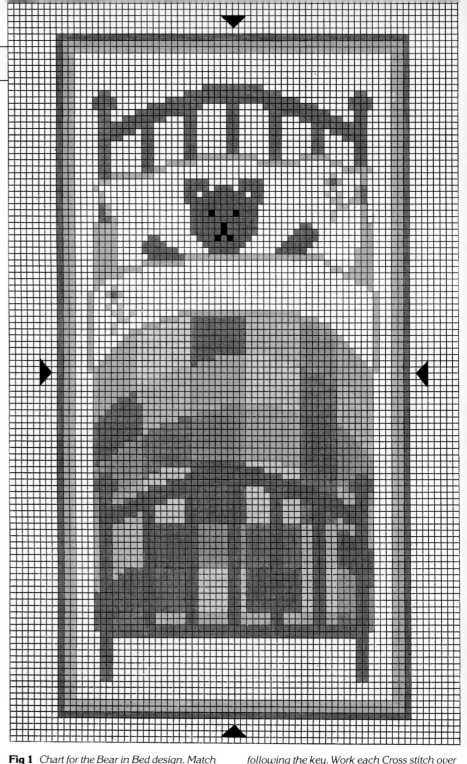

**Fig 1** *Chart for the Bear in Bed design. Match the colours here to the embroidery threads, following the key. Work each Cross stitch over one square of the fabric weave*

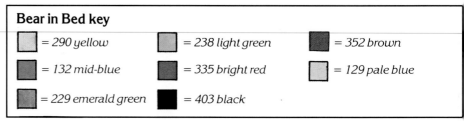

**Bear in Bed key**

| | | |
|---|---|---|
| = 290 yellow | = 238 light green | = 352 brown |
| = 132 mid-blue | = 335 bright red | = 129 pale blue |
| = 229 emerald green | = 403 black | |

Trim the bottom corners diagonally and turn to the right side. Turn a narrow hem on the top edges and then turn and baste a deeper hem to make a casing for the cord. Machine-stitch the casing hem.

## Finishing

Fasten a safety pin to the end of the cord and slip it through the casing. Knot the cord ends together. Pull the cord loop out from the other side of the bag to make two loops (see picture).

# Ideas for the design

The 'Bear in bed' design can be used to make other needlework furnishings. If the design is worked on a soft, evenweave fabric with each Cross stitch 6mm *(¼in)* across, the design would enlarge to approximately 67 × 35cm *(26½ × 14in)* and this would make a charming embroidery for a bed cover.

Worked in rug wool on rug canvas, the same design makes a matching bedside rug. By tracing the pattern (Fig 1) and enlarging it photographically, the 'Bear in bed' could also be used for an appliqué project.

# Chapter Four

# Back Stitch

Back stitch is a very useful stitch and is used primarily for outlining. It can also be used in massed rows to fill an area and, on evenweave fabric, complex linear patterns can be built up. In this chapter, Back stitch is used to embroider curtain ties with a butterfly and ivy design and the same theme is used to work a quilted cushion.

## Butterfly tieback and cushion

Only Back stitch is used for the embroidery, worked along the design lines. The stems of the foliage appear slightly thicker than the other lines (see picture). This is achieved by working two lines of Back stitches in two shades of green thread.

## Tieback

### Materials required

*For one tieback* 3 pieces of firm white cotton fabric 60 × 30cm *(24 × 12in)*

Anchor stranded embroidery cotton as follows: 1 skein each of 205 jade green, 241 pale jade green, 337 pale russet, 339 mid-russet, 110 mid-violet; 2 skeins each of 253 pale green, 95 pale mauve, 305 mid-gold

Crewel needle, size 5

130cm *(52in)* of bright green narrow cord

Sewing thread to match cord

2 small plastic rings

### Preparation

Trace the pattern Fig 1 on pages 44–5, matching the design lines as indicated and re-trace, to produce a complete pattern.

Spread the pattern on a flat surface and place a piece of the cotton fabric on top. Smooth the fabric and hold in place at the edges with strips of adhesive tape.

Trace over the design lines with a fabric transfer pencil (or washable crayon). Remove the fabric with the design traced upon it and place over a second piece of the cotton fabric.

Smooth the layers together and then baste with soft basting thread, starting in the middle and working out to the edges.

Place the mounted fabric in an embroidery hoop, stretching it carefully until the fabric is quite taut. You will only be able to fit part of the design in the hoop to start with, and will need to remove and reposition the fabric several times to complete the design.

## Working the embroidery

Six strands of embroidery cotton are used together throughout the embroidery to give a bold and well-defined line.

Choose any area to begin embroidery and follow the colour key for the correct thread to use. Work even Back stitches (see Figs 1–4, page 45) along all the lines of the design. It may be necessary to work smaller Back stitches at corners or when working small shapes.

Work the butterfly wing outlines before filling in the veins. Work the ivy leaves and continue the stitching into the stems, thickening them slightly by working a second line alongside using a different shade of green.

When the embroidery is completed, remove it from the frame and unpick the basting threads. Press the fabric on the wrong side very lightly, to encourage the stitchery to appear 'embossed' on the right side.

## Making the tieback

Trim the excess fabric away up to the cutting line. Place the embroidery right side down on a piece of the cotton fabric. Pin and baste the layers together along the seam line, 1cm (³/8in) inside the cutting line.

Machine-stitch on the seam line, leaving a gap on a curved edge approximately 10cm (4in) long.

Trim away the surplus fabric and snip into the seam allowance on the curves. Turn the tieback to the right side and press very gently, if necessary.

Close the open seam with tiny-hand sewing stitches.

Make a second tieback in the same way.

Sew the green cord around the edges of the tieback, starting and ending on one of the short sides.

## Making covered rings

Using pale green thread 253, work Buttonhole stitch (see page 56) over the rings until the plastic is covered (see Fig 1 below). Tie the thread ends together.

Sew the covered rings to the middle of each of the tieback's short sides.

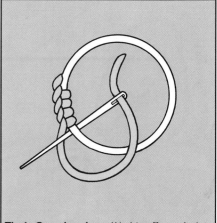

**Fig 1  Covering rings:** *Working Buttonhole stitch exactly as described on page 56 to cover a ring*

# Butterfly motif

The butterfly motif (Fig 2) is a simple linear design and is ideal for practising Back stitch. It can be used to decorate the corner of a traycloth or on a place mat and napkin set. Several butterflies could be worked along the edges of a cotton curtain, or randomly placed on a fabric blind.

Butterflies are also delightful motifs for children's clothes, particularly if a few daisies are added to the design (refer to page 22).

## Butterfly tieback and quilted cushion key

= 253 pale green    = 205 jade green    = 337 pale russet    = 95 pale mauve

= 241 pale jade green    = 305 mid-gold    = 339 mid-russet    = 110 mid-violet

**Fig 1 Curtain tie pattern:** *Trace the pattern piece on folded paper: re-trace to obtain a complete pattern. Join the two segments where they are broken across the middle of the page*

**Fig 2** *Trace the motif and use it for decorating table linens, or work several in a random pattern on curtains or a blind*

**Fig 1**

**Fig 2**

**Fig 3**

**Fig 4**

## Back stitch

In working Back stitch, it is important that every stitch is of exactly the same length and this takes practice to achieve. It is worth trying several lines of Back stitches on scraps of fabric until a smooth and even line of embroidery is worked and then you will be ready to try the butterfly motif.

1. Bring the needle through on the design line at A and insert the needle at B (Fig 1).

2. Bring the needle through at C (exactly the stitch length of A–B) in front of A (Fig 2).

3. Re-insert the needle at A again, in exactly the same hole previously made (Fig 3).

4. Bring the needle through at D (making sure the distance between C–D is the same length as the previous stitches), and insert it at C, in the same hole (Fig 4). Continue making stitches in the same way.

# Quilted cushion

The pretty quilted cushion in the picture on page 42 has the same Butterfly and ivy pattern as the curtain tieback.

Back stitch is used for the quilting and the use of fabric transfer crayons adds delicate colour to the effect.

## Materials required

80cm (32in) of 152cm (60in)-wide white polyester cotton
50cm (20in) square of medium-weight polyester wadding
35cm (14in)-diameter circular cushion pad
Anchor stranded embroidery cotton as follows: 1 skein each of 337 pale russet, 305 mid-gold, 110 mid-violet, 241 pale jade green, 205 jade green
Crewel needle, size 7
White sewing thread
50cm (20in)-square piece of tracing paper
Fabric transfer crayons
45cm (18in)-square wooden embroidery frame (for mounting the fabric)

## Preparation

Spread out the white cotton fabric and measure and cut off two strips each measuring 15cm (6in) by the width of the fabric (152cm (60in)).

Put these aside for the cushion frill.

Measure and cut the remaining fabric into three squares, each 50cm (20in)-square. Put one of these aside for the cushion back. Stretch one of the remaining squares over the wooden frame, aligning the sides of the frame with the straight grain of fabric. This is important to prevent the fabric becoming distorted.

On the sheet of tracing paper, draw a circle with a radius of 17cm (6³⁄₄in). This will be the seam line of the finished cushion. (If you prefer, you can draw the circle by tracing the quarter segment of the cushion pattern given (Fig 1), moving the paper and re-tracing the segments to obtain the complete circle.) Place the tracing paper over the pattern (Fig 1), matching the seam line with the broken line. Using fabric transfer crayons, lightly colour in the design. As each quarter-segment is coloured, re-align the tracing paper

until the complete pattern is obtained.

Be careful not to smudge the crayonned surface as the tracing paper is moved, as this will show on the fabric later. Try to use the crayons smoothly so that an even spread of colour is achieved.

Press the second piece of fabric to remove any creases. Place the crayonned paper face down on the fabric, centring it. Press very carefully with an iron to transfer and fix the design on fabric. (Follow the manufacturer's instructions for the heat of the iron.)

Great care must be taken not to move the paper while pressing as this will blur and distort the image.

Place the wadding over the stretched fabric in the frame and spread the printed fabric on top, right side up. Make sure that the straight grain of the printed fabric aligns with the sides of the frame.

Pin the three layers together at the sides of the frame. To do this, press the layers down with one hand and smooth the top fabric and wadding towards the side of the frame with the other. Insert

the pins. Repeat this process on the opposite side of the frame and then work the two remaining sides. The wadding should be firmly 'sandwiched' between the layers of fabric.

## Working the embroidery

Three strands of embroidery cotton are used throughout the embroidery.

Following the instructions for working Back stitch on page 45, work even Back stitches on all the lines of the design, through all the thicknesses of fabric. The colour key for the cushion is the same as for the tieback (see page 44).

Work the inner parts of the design first and then work outwards towards the edges. Work round the leaves and butterflies before adding details of veins, antennae, etc.

The lines of Back stitches will 'pinch' the wadding around the wings and leaves so that they appear to be padded and 'embossed'.

When all the embroidery is completed, baste around the seam line using white sewing thread. (Use the paper pattern as a guide.) Remove the quilted fabric from the frame.

**Fig 1 Quilted butterfly cushion:** *One-quarter of the round cushion pattern. Trace the shape on a square piece of paper then move the paper and re-trace the shape, joining design lines at the edges so that a complete circular pattern is obtained*

Cut 1cm (³⁄₈in) from the seam line.

**Making the cushion**

Join the two strips of fabric on the short ends to make a ring of fabric. Fold along the length, matching the raw edges and with wrong sides together. Work two rows of gathering stitches through the raw edges. Carefully draw up the gathering threads to fit the frill along the seam line of the cushion. Fasten off the gathering threads with a small Back stitch and then pin the frill to the right side of the cushion along the seam line, matching raw edges. Baste with small stitches so that the gathers are held evenly. Machine-stitch through the gathers leaving a 15cm (6in) gap in the seam. Remove the basting thread.

Place the remaining piece of fabric on the cushion, right sides together so that the frill lies to the middle. Pin and baste the layers together on the stitched seam line. Machine-stitch on the same seam line as before, leaving a 15cm (6in) gap in the seam. Remove the basting threads. Trim away the surplus fabric. If you prefer, the raw edges of the seam allowance can be oversewn together to neaten them (refer to page 14). Turn the cushion cover to the right side.

Insert the cushion pad through the gap in the seam. Fold in the raw edges and hand-sew with small stitches, using white sewing thread.

# Chapter Five

# Chain Stitch

During the previous chapters, you have worked Straight stitches in a variety of ways and you are now ready to learn a more complicated stitch – Chain stitch. This is one of the many loop stitches and it can be used in different ways: as an outlining stitch, as a filling stitch and in flower-like groups. In this chapter, you are shown how to work simple apple motifs on a place mat, tray cloth and on children's play clothes, and then how to create a Forget-me-not tablecloth and napkins.

## Apple place mat

Place mats and tray cloths are a good way of displaying your embroidery expertise – and an opportunity for practising new stitches. Linen-weave place mats can be purchased ready-made in many department stores and, decorated with a simple embroidery motif, become a personalised home furnishing.

The apple (Fig 1) is designed as a practice piece for Chain stitch and it should take a beginner just over an hour to complete.

### Materials required
Yellow linen-weave place mat
Piece of thin cardboard for a template
Embroidery transfer pencil
DMC Coton Perlé No. 5 as follows:
    1 skein 704 green
Crewel needle, size 5

### Preparation
Trace the apple outline and leaves from Fig 1, ignoring the 'bite' shape for this project. Rub soft pencil over the wrong side of the tracing. Lay the tracing on thin card and draw over the lines with a sharp pencil. Cut out the apple shape and the leaf shapes.

### Using templates
On the place mat pictured, the apple is positioned 3.5cm *(1¼in)* from the bottom hem edge and 4.5cm *(1¾in)* from the right-hand hem edge. Place the apple template on the fabric and hold it down with the fingers. Draw round with an embroidery transfer pencil. Draw in the short stalk free hand.

Then place the leaf templates against the stem on the right and left of the stalk and draw round it.

### Working the embroidery
This embroidery can be worked freely in the hand without a hoop if preferred.

Using the Coton Perlé and following the diagrams (Figs 1–4, page 50), work Chain stitch round the apple outline, making the stitches even in size. Work the short stalk next and then the two leaves, each with a central vein leading into the apple stalk. Finish each line of Chain stitches as described for Detached Chain stitch, Fig 5, page 50.

The motif can be repeated on other mats to make a set, or you may wish to extend the idea by working several motifs around a tablecloth, using the single apple on napkins.

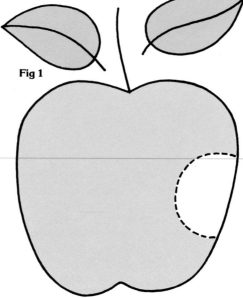

**Fig 1**

**Fig 1** *Trace the apple shape on the solid line for the Apple place mat. Trace the leaves. For Eve's Apple cloth, trace the apple with the bite out of it*

# Eve's apple cloth

The same apple motif is used on the green-checked cloth pictured on the previous page but this time Chain stitches have been used to fill the area, with rows of stitches worked close together.

The fabric for the cloth is, in fact, a dishtowel, which you can buy already hemmed. Embroidered with bright apples, the towel makes a cloth for a small table or a tray cloth.

You can use the same templates that you made for the place mat, but cut a 'bite' from the apple, following the dotted line on the pattern, Fig 1, page 48.

## Materials required

Green and white checked dishtowel
Anchor Pearl cotton No. 5 as follows: 1
  skein each 333 red, 225 and 254 green
Thin cardboard for a template
Crewel needle, size 5

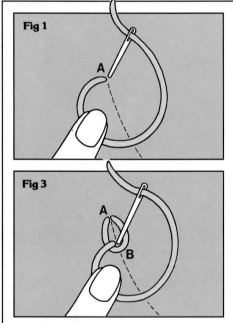

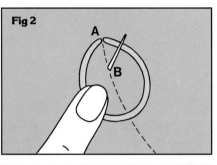

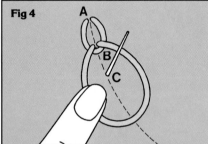

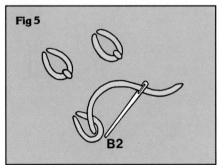

## Chain stitch

Chain stitch is an interesting and absorbing stitch to work but it does take time to learn how to get the loops gently curved and of even size. Practise with soft embroidery cotton on a piece of medium-weight fabric – or even a clean dishtowel – until you can work a perfectly formed line of stitches.
1.  Bring the needle through at A and, while holding the thread down with the thumb (see Fig 1), insert the needle into the same hole at A (Fig 1).
2.  Bring the needle through at B, a short distance in front of A, and coming up through the loop of thread (see Fig 2). The thumb still holds the thread down.
3.  As the needle is pulled through, the thread tightens and the chain begins to be formed. When the chain is properly formed, re-insert the needle into the same hole, B, the thumb holding the thread down for the next chain (Fig 3).
4.  Bring the needle through at C, the same distance as A–B in front of B (Fig 4).

Re-insert the needle into C to form the next chain, the thumb still holding down the loop of thread exactly as in Fig 3. This procedure will form a continuous line of Chain stitches.
5. For a Detached Chain stitch, refer back to Fig 2, bringing the thread through at B. Pull the thread through to form the loop, then insert the needle at B2, outside the loop. This makes a tying stitch which holds the loop secure (Fig 5). This stitch is also used to finish off a continuous row of Chain stitches.

## Preparation

Make the template using the thin cardboard as described for the apple place mat (page 48) and draw the apple and leaves onto each corner of the dishtowel.

The apple can have the 'bite' facing the same direction in all four corners, or you can reverse the template so that the 'bite' is on the other side of the apple.

You will find it easier to work the motifs if the fabric is stretched and held taut in an embroidery hoop, as if filled shapes of solid stitchery are worked without a hoop there is a risk of your pulling the stitchery too tightly, causing the flatness of the fabric to become distorted.

Using the red thread and referring to the Chain stitch diagrams, stitch round the apple shape on the design outline. When you arrive back at the starting point, continue working Chain stitches along the inside of the previous line of Chain stitches, and work as close to this as possible.

Continue working round inside the apple shape with this continuous line of Chain stitches until it is completely filled.

Work a single line of Chain stitches for the stalk, using the lighter green thread. Use the same shade to work the centre vein of each leaf, and then fill in the upper halves of the leaves. Use the darker green shade to fill the lower half.

You will find the easiest method of filling in each half leaf shape is to work from the stalk end to the tip along the drawn outer line, and then work filling lines of stitches on the inside so that you are working in towards the stitched vein line.

# Happy apple suit

The child's shirt and play trousers pictured were purchased separately, but by decorating the garments with embroidery a charming, co-ordinated outfit is achieved.

## Materials required

Purchased play trousers and short-sleeved shirt with collar
Dressmaker's carbon paper
Thin card for a template
Anchor stranded embroidery cotton as follows: 1 skein each of 333 red, 225 emerald and 264 pale olive
Crewel needle, size 7

## Preparation

Trace the small apple motif and the tiny leaf spray (Fig 1).

Trace the apple with the bite out of it from Fig 1, page 48.

Make a card template for the larger apple.

Trace the small apple onto one of the shirt's collar points using dressmaker's carbon paper. Reverse the tracing for the apple on the other collar point, so that they are symmetrical. Transfer five leaf sprays around the collar, spacing them equidistantly (see picture).

Using the template, draw round the shape on the bib of the play trousers, adding two leaves and a stalk. Using dressmaker's carbon paper, transfer leaf sprays to the straps of the play trousers (see picture).

## Working the embroidery

**Shirt** Work the shirt first, holding the garment freely in the hand for embroidery.

Using three strands of thread throughout, work the small apples in red thread using Chain stitches (see opposite). The stitches are very small for this project (see detail). Work the outlines first, then fill in with stitches, working round inside the shape.

Using the darker green thread, work the apple stalk with about six Chain stitches.

The leaves are single, larger Chain stitches, set either side of the stalk. When working these, it is important not to pull the thread too tightly, as this will produce a thin-looking leaf. If the thread

is allowed to loop naturally, a gently-curved leaf shape will appear.

Work the leaf sprays round the collar in the same way.

**Play trousers** The leaf sprays on the straps can be worked freely in the hand but a hoop is advised for working the large apple on the bib, as this will prevent the fabric puckering while you are working the massed area of stitchery. If, however, a hoop is not available, you must be very careful with your work to see that the tension of the stitches is even throughout.

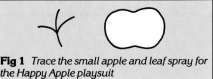

**Fig 1** *Trace the small apple and leaf spray for the Happy Apple playsuit*

Embroider the apple with Chain stitches, following the same method described for Eve's apple cloth. The stalk is a single row of Chain stitches and the two leaves are worked using both shades of green (see detail).

For a finishing touch, sew matching red buttons to the shirt and the bib of the play trousers.

# Forget-me-not table linen

In this Chain stitch project, the design uses lines of Chain stitches for the flower stems, with single or detached Chain stitches for the small leaves. Groups of detached Chain stitches make the forget-me-not flower heads and when used in this way they are called Lazy Daisy stitches.

This is an opportunity for you to use your own sense of creativity in embroidery by positioning the flower heads and tiny leaves where you would like to see them.

## Materials required

*For a 150cm (60in)-square tablecloth and 4 napkins (purchased)*
DMC Coton Perlé No. 5 as follows: 1 skein of white; 2 skeins of 743 and 742 yellows; 4 skeins each of 955, 369 and 913 greens; 4 skeins each of 747, 813 and 800 blues
Tracing paper
Coloured crayons
Crewel needle, size 7

## Preparation

Trace the pattern (Fig 1, page 54). Spread the tracing on a flat surface and place each of the napkins on top, in turn. Trace the design using a fabric transfer pencil.

Trace the posy of flowers onto the corners of the tablecloth and then re-position the cloth to trace a complete border of the intertwined design lines, linking the posies. The areas of the border between arrows are repeated to the length of border required.

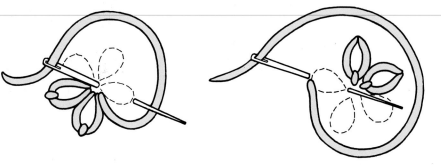

## Lazy Daisies

Lazy Daisy stitches are worked in a circular formation, the stitches radiating from a central point. The basic stitch is Chain stitch.

For Lazy Daisy stitch, the needle is re-inserted in the same central hole to begin each petal (Fig 1).

The stitch can also be used so that the knots are towards the middle of the flower and this produces a pointed rather than a rounded petal (Fig 2).

**Fig 1**

**Fig 2**

## Working the embroidery

A 20cm *(8in)*-diameter embroidery hoop is recommended for working the tablecloth and napkins, as this will prevent the fabric puckering and make the stitching easier.

Using each of the three shades of green thread, work the posy stems. Balance the use of each colour to please yourself. Scatter a few Detached Chain stitches along the stems to represent small leaves.

Work the intertwined lines which form the border and, using the paler greens, scatter small Detached Chain stitched leaves along them at intervals. Refer to Fig 5, page 50 for Detached Chain stitches.

Work the clusters of forget-me-not flowers around the stem heads using the three blue shades of thread (see picture).

Scatter flowers randomly along the intertwined lines. Finish each flower with a small Detached Chain stitch in its centre, using one of the yellow threads.

To finish, cut two lengths of the white Coton Perlé, each measuring 15cm *(6in)* long and, threading the lengths into the needle, weave them through the Chain stitches, down one side of the embroidered stalks of each posy and up the other so that the two loose ends are on the right side of the fabric. Then tie the ends into a small neat bow (see picture).

Work the tablecloth posies and intertwined border in the same way.

**Fig 1** *Trace-off pattern for the Forget-me-not table napkin. Trace the flower spray separately for the tablecloth corners, then repeat the sections of intertwined border between arrows for the tablecloth border*

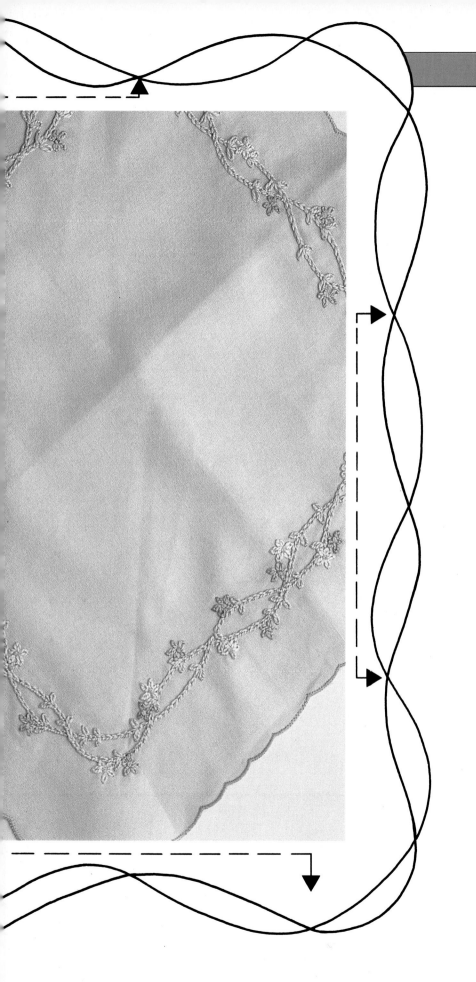

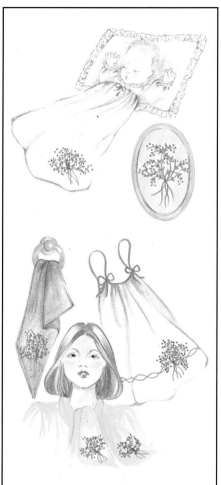

# Ideas for flower motifs

Flower sprays have many applications in embroidery, both for home items and for garments and accessories. The corner spray on the Forget-me-not table linen has been worked entirely in Chain stitches but, if you prefer, other stitches could be used instead – such as Satin stitch, French knots and Stem stitch.

The motif would look charming on bed linens, perhaps on the corner of the top sheet and on the pillow cases, worked white on white, or white on pastel colours.

It could also be used on the four corners of a cushion, or be worked on guest towels. Worked in a range of bright pastel shades, the spray makes a pretty picture perhaps framed with an oval mount.

In fashion, try the motif on a blouse or dress front, or on the ends of a silky scarf and it is the ideal size for embroidering on lingerie or night wear. Repeated and linked with the ribbon border, the spray would also look pretty around the hem of a long baby gown.

# Chapter Six

# Buttonhole Stitch

There is no real difference between Buttonhole stitch and Blanket stitch. The former is worked so that the stitches lie close together and the latter has stitches spaced evenly apart. Both variations are in this chapter, where you are given an appliqué motif for bathroom towels, ideas for decorating table linen with motifs abstracted from a teaset, and a pretty camisole top to make with cutwork decoration.

## Appliquéd bathroom towel

The technique used to decorate the towel pictured is called 'appliqué'. This is where a motif is applied with stitches to the background fabric.

This popular – and easy – embroidery technique has many applications, from children's clothes to high fashion, and from small room accessories to larger items like bed covers, quilts and curtains. (See Chapter Ten.)

Blanket stitch has been used here to apply the motifs but Buttonhole stitch and machine-worked Satin stitch are both used for appliqué, depending on the item being made.

Before starting an appliqué project, make sure that both the background fabric and the appliqué fabric are colourfast and have been pre-shrunk. If you are not sure, wash them both.

### Materials required
*To apply 1 motif to a towel*
Plain white towel
15cm *(6in)* square of lavender blue cotton fabric
15cm *(6in)* square of pale green cotton fabric
Anchor stranded embroidery cotton as follows: 1 skein each of 130 blue, 241 pale jade green, 01 white, 06 peach
Basting thread
Crewel needle, size 7
15 × 30cm *(6 × 12in)* piece of lightweight iron-on interfacing

*Note:* if you are decorating a set of towels, bathtowels or handtowels, you will need additional fabric and interfacing and, possibly, extra embroidery thread.

## Buttonhole stitch

Both Buttonhole stitch and Blanket stitch are worked from left to right and success depends on keeping the stitches upright and even in length.

1. Bring the needle through on the bottom design line A. Insert the needle at B on the top design line and slightly to the right (Fig 1). Bring the needle out at C directly below B. Before pulling the needle through, take the thread under the needle point.
2. Pull the needle through to form the stitch. Insert the needle at D on the top design line and bring it out at E, immediately below, with the thread under the needle point as shown in Fig 2.
3. Pull the needle and thread through and then continue to make stitches in the same way, very close together (Fig 3).
4. Blanket stitch is worked in exactly the same way but stitches are spaced equidistantly apart (Fig 4).

You may find it difficult at first to make this stitch successfully because it is all too easy to pull the thread too tightly and so fail to get a 'right-angled' stitch. Practice is important to achieve the right tension and, while you are practising, try out stitches of different lengths and with different spacings. You will be interested to see how many variations can be achieved with a single stitch.

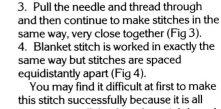

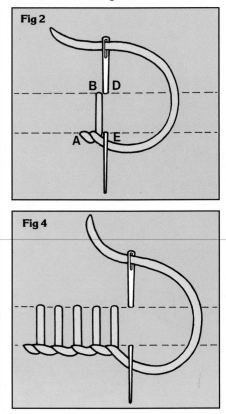

▶

## Preparation

Trace the flower and leaf shapes from Fig 1 onto paper and cut out on the solid lines to make paper patterns. Pin the patterns to the fabrics and cut out one flower from the blue fabric and two leaves from the green fabric. (Repeat this if you are cutting out more flowers.)

Trace the broken line on your paper patterns from Fig 1. Cut out on the broken line. Use the patterns to cut shapes from iron-on interfacing (making sure that the adhesive side of the interfacing is uppermost). Again, cut one flower and two leaf shapes.

Following the manufacturer's instructions, press the interfacing shapes to the wrong side of the fabric shapes, centring them.

Using a pair of small, sharply-pointed scissors, snip into the edge of each shape towards the interfacing. The cuts enable you to fold the small turning neatly onto the wrong side. Work basting stitches to hold the turning (Fig 2).

Arrange the flower and leaves on one corner of the towel with the flower overlapping the leaves slightly (see picture).

Pin and then baste the shapes to the towel.

## Working the embroidery

The embroidery can be worked freely in the hand without the use of a hoop.

Using three strands of embroidery cotton, work Blanket stitches (see Fig 4, page 56) around the flower and leaf edges. Try to make each stitch 3mm ($^1/_8$in) in length and space them 3mm ($^1/_8$in) apart – but if stitches are longer than this and wider apart it does not matter as long as they are regular and even. Where the flower overlaps the leaves there is extra thickness of fabric and extra care must be taken with stitchery at this point.

When the shapes are applied, remove the basting stitches.

Using green thread, work lines on the leaves using either Back stitch (page 45) or Chain stitch (page 50).

Using peach thread and Back stitch, work radiating lines from the centre of the flower (Fig 1). Work a single small detached Chain stitch (page 50) in white at the end of each line.

When working embroidery stitches on appliqué, remember that you do not

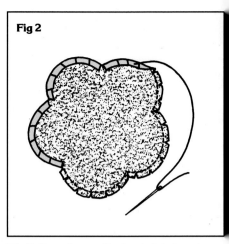

**Fig 2** *Preparing appliqué: snip into the edges and turn to the wrong side. Baste to hold the turning*

have to take stitching through the towel, as the motifs are already firmly attached with Blanket stitching. Work the stitches through the surface layer of fabric only.

## Finishing

The towel pictured has a woven border running across the towel and this has been edged with Blanket stitches in green thread for a finishing touch.

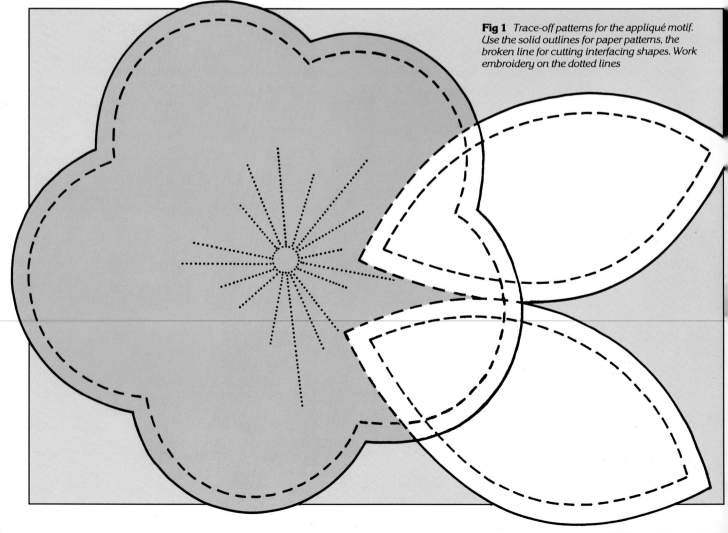

**Fig 1** *Trace-off patterns for the appliqué motif. Use the solid outlines for paper patterns, the broken line for cutting interfacing shapes. Work embroidery on the dotted lines*

# Camisole with cutwork

Buttonhole stitch is used for the type of embroidery called 'cutwork'. In this technique, areas of the pattern are bordered with Buttonhole stitches and the background fabric is cut away. Traditionally, cutwork was worked on white fabric with white embroidery but modern cutwork often has pretty, colourful effects, as can be seen in the camisole pictured.

The camisole was made from a commercial paper pattern, using a finely woven cotton fabric with a woven satin dot.

## Materials required

Plain white camisole top with a
    scooped neckline
DMC stranded embroidery cotton as
    follows: 1 skein each of 819 pale
    pink, 775 pale blue, 369 pale green
Crewel needle, size 7
Pale blue satin ribbon 3mm (1/8in) wide
    for straps (optional)
Matching coloured crayons

## Preparation

Measure and mark the centre of the neckline with basting stitches.

Trace the design (Fig 1) directly onto the fabric using sharply-pointed crayons in colours close to the embroidery threads. Position the motif about 15mm (5/8in) below the neckline edge.

## Working the embroidery

The embroidery is worked freely in the hand.

Using three strands of embroidery thread throughout, work Buttonhole stitch (page 56) on all the design lines, referring to the picture. Work all the stitches so that the knots lie on the solid lines of the design. Use the broken line as a guide to the length of the stitch.

Work the flowers in pale pink, the leaves and flower centres in pale green and the triangle in pale blue.

## Working cutwork

With a very sharp pair of pointed scissors, cut away the fabric areas which are shown as blue on Fig 1. The edges must be smooth and neat but care must be taken to see that the

**Fig 1**

*Design line to be traced onto fabric*

*Guideline to show width of stitch (do not transfer to fabric)*

*Areas to be cut away when stitchery is complete*

stitches are not cut.

You will find it easier to cut away a shape if you pierce the blade of the scissors into the middle of the area and then, very carefully, cut towards the line of Buttonhole stitches. Cut close to the stitches but do not damage them.

When all the work has been

completed, press the camisole gently on the wrong side to make the stitching stand out.

## Finishing

If desired, the camisole can be given straps of pale blue satin ribbon, finished with tiny stitched bows.

**Fig 1** *Trace the design from the chinaware and simplify the lines and shapes*

**Fig 2** *The design is simplified even further for working in appliqué and embroidery*

# Embroidery patterns from chinaware

Inspiration for embroidery designs is to be found all about you, but one of the most obvious sources of potential embroidery motifs lies in furnishing fabrics, wallpapers and one's own chinaware.

The tray mat and napkin in the picture have an appliqué and embroidery design on them which has been abstracted from a teaset. Co-ordinated china and table linen has considerable eye-appeal and makes a good conversation point.

## Designing from china

If some of the areas of design are going to be interpreted into appliqué, they need to be simplified. Fig 1 shows the design of the china pattern pictured and Fig 2 shows it simplified for appliqué. When translated into thread, the larger flowers are appliquéd with Buttonhole stitch while the remaining, smaller flowers and leaves are worked in detached Chain stitches, Straight stitches, Back stitches and French knots.

Select a fairly large plate from the set of china and trace the design as carefully as possible. Spread your

tracing out before you and study it.

You will probably feel the line is rather shaky and in need of 'tidying up'. Do this by redrawing or tracing over the shapes, smoothing lines and possibly simplifying some areas in order to make it more suitable for stitchery.

Rearrange the motifs into the shape required to fit the table linen. For example, you may wish to straighten the curved border of a plate so that it will fit along the straight edge of a tray cloth – as has been done with the tea set border.

Next, decide which areas are to be appliquéd and then decide how you can best interpret the rest of the design.

You can always practise your stitches on a small scrap of fabric – even an old handkerchief – in order to choose which stitches look best.

Once you have decided how to work the design, prepare the appliqué shapes. In this project the shapes are prepared in a different way to that of the appliqué towel project (page 56), where the raw edges of shapes were turned to the wrong side and then evenly shaped Blanket stitches were used to attach the motif to the towel.

## Preparing for appliqué

Cut out the paper patterns without a turning allowance. Bond the fabrics to the iron-on interfacing. Using the paper patterns, cut out the motifs, with no allowance for turnings.

Pin the fabric shapes in position on the table linen, carefully re-arranging and adjusting until you are satisfied that they are correctly placed. Use the original tracing of the design to help you, by placing it over the arrangement and adjusting the appliqué shapes as necessary underneath.

Pin, then baste the shapes in place.

Using three strands of embroidery cotton, work a neat line of Buttonhole stitch (Figs 1–3, page 56) around each shape so that the knots of the stitches lie on the outer edge of each shape, with the 'arms' of the stitches closely protecting the raw edge of the appliqué shape (Fig 3 opposite).

The line of Buttonhole stitching should look smooth and be of even tension.

Work around all the appliqué shapes and then, using different coloured threads and the most appropriate stitch, work the remaining areas of embroidery.

As you can see from the picture, in the example of embroidery worked stitches, threads and fabrics have been thoughtfully chosen, as the design has simple shapes.

The stems and small flower centres are worked in a deep rose colour, the stems being interpreted in Back stitch (see page 45) and small French knots.

The blue petals of the small flowers are detached Chain stitches or Lazy Daisy stitches (see page 52).

The leaves are worked in two shades of moss green in long Straight stitches (see page 18) to fill in the leaf shape and give an effect of shading which closely follows the design on the china.

When all the stitchery is completed, press the table linen gently on the wrong side to encourage the stitchery to stand out on the right side.

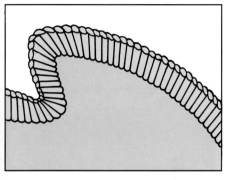

**Fig 3** *Work Buttonhole stitch on the appliqué edges, so that the knots lie on the outer edge*

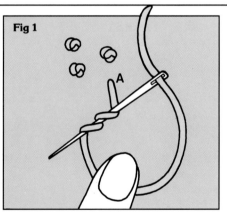

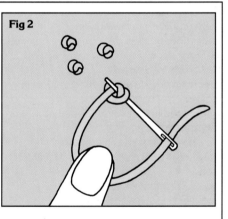

## French knots

French knots can be used singly as spots in a design and are often used for the stamens of flowers.

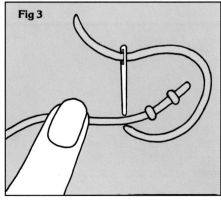

1. Bring the needle through at A (where the knot is desired) and wind the thread round the needle twice as shown (Fig 1).
2. Holding the thread down with the thumb, twist the needle back to A and insert if where it first came out (Fig 2). Holding the knot down with the thumb, pull the thread through from the back and secure the knot on the wrong side.

## Couching

A thread is laid along the fabric surface and held down while a different needle and thread works small holding stitches over it at intervals (Fig 3).

# Mixed Stitches

With the stitches you have learned so far, a whole new world of embroidery opens up before you and, as your expertise grows, so will your confidence in undertaking more complicated pieces. In this chapter, there is a cushion to work in crewel wools, a miniature picture to embroider, a Persian patterned scarf and some ideas for making a needlework 'portrait' of your home. Finally, there are ideas for 'scribbling' on a T-shirt and two motifs with which to embellish clothes.

## Crewel-work cushion

Crewel embroidery is the name given to a free-flowing style of design (usually floral), worked in two-ply lightly twisted wool on linen, twill or satinised cotton fabric. A variety of stitches are traditionally used in crewel work, and shading with Long and Short stitches is one of the features of the embroidery.

The cushion pictured is a modern interpretation of crewel work (sometimes called Jacobean embroidery).

### Materials required
*Size: 35cm (14in)-square cushion*
45 × 90cm *(18 × 36in)* piece of satinised embroidery fabric in a natural shade
Paterna Persian yarn as follows:
2 skeins each of 923, 924, 925 wood rose, 513, 514, 515 old blue, 523, 524, 525 teal blue
Chenille needle, size 18
Cushion pad

### Preparation
Cut the fabric into two pieces, each 45cm *(18in)* square. Put one aside for the cushion back.

Enlarge the design (Fig 1) photo-graphically to 28cm *(11in)* across. Trace the photographic print and draw over the lines on the wrong side with an embroidery transfer pencil. Following the manufacturer's instructions, transfer the design to the fabric.

Alternatively, trace the design onto the fabric using dressmaker's carbon paper.

### Working the embroidery
The detail shows the way in which the

**Fig 1** *Pattern for the crewel-work cushion. Enlarge this photographically and then trace for a pattern*

colour shading has been worked on the flowers and leaves. Long and Short stitches (see page 28) are worked to achieve this effect and the length of the stitches can be adjusted to fit a shape.

Begin with the darker yarn shades and work towards the edges of shapes using the medium tone and then the lightest colour. The large flower has petals shaded in the pink yarns, with

Buttonhole stitch (page 56) petals in the centre worked in old blue shades.

Detached Chain stitches (Fig 5, page 50) in dark pink are worked in the centre of each blue petal.

The smaller flowers are worked in old blue yarns, the darker shade towards the middle of each petal, with the lighter shades at the outside edges of the flower. French knots (page 61) in dark pink are grouped in the centres.

The stems and inner leaves are worked in Stem stitch (below) using the medium leaf yarn. The leaves are shaded in the three leaf yarns.

The smaller leaves are worked with Long and Short stitches in the light leaf yarn on one side and outlined with a darker tone on the other. Small French knots in the darker shade are worked in a row to represent the leaf vein.

To add texture to the embroidery, a leaf stem and the stem of the large flower have been further embellished by needle-weaving a lighter leaf thread through the stitchery.

## Making the cushion

Do not press wool embroidery, as this may flatten the stitches.

Trim the embroidered fabric back to 38cm (15in)-square, keeping the embroidery centred. Trim the cushion back to the same size.

Place the front and back together right sides facing. Pin and baste on three sides. Machine-stitch taking a 12mm (½in) seam. Trim the corners diagonally and turn to the right side.

Insert the cushion pad and close the open seam with hand-sewing.

## Finishing

Twist a cord from the remaining blue yarns and sew it round the cushion, tying the ends in a knot at one corner. Fringe the knot ends. (Refer to page 17 for the technique of making cords.)

# Persian-patterned scarf

The rich colours and flowing floral design worked on this wool scarf were inspired by the pattern of an old Persian embroidery. Here the border pattern is worked on two sides of a square but it could be repeated to go on all four sides if desired.

The scale of the design makes it suitable for larger items also, such as a bed cover or a room divider curtain.

Fig 1 on page 66 is the corner motif which could be repeated round the sides of a square or rectangle. Fig 2 (page 67) is a finishing motif such as that used for the ends of the border on the scarf.

### Materials required

*Finished size 60cm (24in) square*
60cm (24in) square of finely woven wool fabric
Fabric transfer pencil
DMC Laine Medicis as follows: 1 skein each of 8103 red, 8129 salmon, 8139 light salmon, 8505A very pale salmon, 8328 very pale yellow, 8327 mustard yellow, 8402 grass green, 8415 dark green
Tapestry needle, size 20
Turquoise sewing thread (optional)

### Preparation

Trace the pattern from Figs 1 and 2 (pages 66–7) to make a border and then draw over the lines on the wrong side of the tracing with a fabric transfer pencil.

Following the manufacturer's instructions, transfer the design onto the fabric so that it is positioned along two adjoining sides.

### Working the embroidery

An embroidery hoop should be used for working this project.

Use three strands of wool together throughout.

Work the stems of the trailing plants in Stem stitch (left) using grass green yarn.

Work the inner leaves in the darker green and the other leaves in grass green using Long and Short stitches (page 28).

The flowers are worked in Long and Short stitches, each using three different colours and you may use your own creativity in deciding what these colours should be.

# Stem stitch

1. Bring the thread through on the design line at A and hold it down with the thumb as shown in Fig 1. Insert the needle at B and bring it out at C, halfway between A and B.

Pull the needle and thread through to set the first stitch. Holding the thread down with the thumb (see Fig 2) insert the needle at D (exactly the same distance as A–C from where the thread emerges) and bring it out at B.

3. Insert the needle at E and bring it out at D (Fig 3). Continue making stitches in this way.

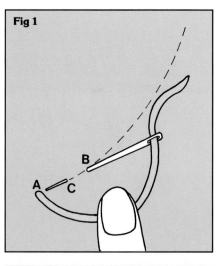

Fig 1

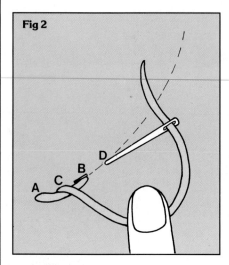

Fig 2

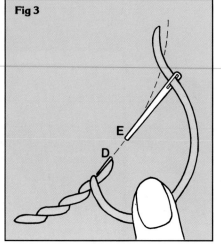

Fig 3

## Finishing

To finish the scarf with a fringe, either work a row of machine-stitching using matching sewing thread 4cm *(1½in)* from the raw edge, or work a row of Back stitches (page 45) in mustard yellow yarn. Pull threads from the fabric edge to make a 4cm *(1½in)* fringe.

# Ideas for the motif

The flower spray in the Persian pattern design is fairly open and can therefore be used for different embroidery techniques. For instance, it could be used as a quilting pattern for a purse or belt, or for a long padded waistcoat.

The design might also be worked in outline stitches for table linens — try the effects of outlining the pattern in Stem stitch or Back stitch, worked as a border on a tablecloth.

**Fig 1** *The corner motif of the pattern. Join pattern lines where they break in the middle of the page*

## Fly stitch

Bring the needle through at A, insert it at B and bring it out again at C. Work a couching stitch over the loop to hold it and then take the needle to the next position for another Fly stitch.

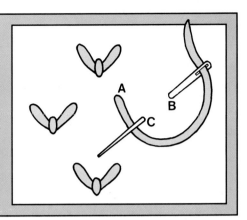

The Persian border is designed to be worked on two sides of a small scarf, using the Fig 1 corner and the Fig 2 end motif. It can be extended to any length, for a shawl, or can be worked on all four edges of a larger piece, such as a quilt or curtain.

**Fig 2** Use this motif at the ends of the Fig 1 corner motif to complete the scarf design

# Miniature in embroidery

This small embroidered picture is the first project where you begin to use a wide variety of the stitches with which you are now familiar. You will see how their different shapes can be used together to give different effects and how these in turn can be used to build up a simple but beautiful image.

Again, the use of fabric transfer crayons gives the background colour on which to build the areas of stitchery.

The idea for this project came from looking at a view of gardens photographed as colour transparencies.

A fabric frame shaped like a transparency mount would be an attractive and unusual way of displaying this type of embroidery picture. Cut a frame shape from pelmet-weight interfacing and cover it with fabric in a complementary colour. Glue the finished embroidery behind the frame. Sew on a small ring for hanging.

## Materials required
25 × 50cm *(10 × 20in)* piece of white polycotton fabric
DMC stranded embroidery cotton as follows: 1 skein each of 702 mid green, 954 pale jade, 955 very pale jade, 809 pale blue, 775 very pale blue, 211 pale mauve, 402 rust, 754 salmon
Crewel needle, size 7
1 packet fabric transfer crayons

## Preparation
Place a piece of tracing paper over the picture and trace off the general outlines. Very lightly crayon in the areas as evenly as possible. Do not press hard, as this gives very strong colours and the effect you want to achieve is one of light, delicate shading.

Fold the piece of white polycotton in half to give a double layer measuring 25 × 25cm *(10 × 10in)*. Iron the folded fabric to remove any creases.

Transfer the crayonned design onto the fabric, following the manufacturer's instructions.

Place the doubled layer of fabric into a wooden embroidery hoop 20cm *(8in)* in diameter, stretching the fabric to achieve a taut area within the hoop.

## Working the embroidery
Use three strands of embroidery cotton throughout the stitchery.

Work the outer arch in two rows of the darker rust shade and one row of the paler rust shade using Back stitch (page 45).

Work the inner arch in one row of the darker rust and one row in paler rust, side by side, again in Back stitch.

The gate is also worked in Back stitch, using the darker rust shade throughout, working three lines of stitches close to one another for each gate post and then single lines for the cross bars.

Using the two paler shades of green, work small groups of Detached Chain stitches (see Fig 5, page 50) along the outer arch to represent small clumps of leaves.

Using the two deeper shades of green, work the leaves in clumps around the inner arch.

Using only the very pale green, scatter tiny Detached Chain stitches all over the lightly-coloured hedge archway. The tiny stitches should be made so that they face in all directions to form a random covering of surface texture.

Using the three shades of green thread, work the small clumps of foliage in the foreground in Back stitch. Work groups of mauve and blue Detached Chain stitches so that they look like tiny flowers.

Finally, around the outer arch, scatter a few tiny light blue Detached Chain stitches and then a few deeper blue Chain stitches (page 50) around the inner arch.

# Scribble on a T-shirt

You can embroider a T-shirt with lines and swirls of embroidery for a distinctive fashion look using just one stitch – Chain stitch, the stitches massed in rows for a bold effect.

Use soft embroidery cotton or Pearl cotton and a crewel needle, size 7.

Cotton jersey tends to stretch during working and you may find it helps to work over a pillow. Pin brown paper round the pillow closely and slip the T-shirt onto it, so that the fabric is supported.

Sketch design lines with a piece of chalk or crayon (or wear the T-shirt and get a friend to scribble on you!).

## Key to embroidery

A  Three single rows of Chain stitch in orange, green and mauve

B  Four rows of Chain stitch in purple, three rows in green, and two rows in orange

C  Four lines of Chain stitch crossed, each line with three rows in blue, pink, mauve and green

D  Lines of three rows in Chain stitch, with Buttonhole-stitched edging in mauve and green

E  Three single curved rows of Chain stitch in green, mauve and orange

F  Three lines of Chain stitch crossed, each line with two rows, in blue, pink and purple

G  Three rows of Chain stitch worked in a spiral with two rows superimposed on the third in a twisted line, in gold, purple and mauve. A bow is sewn on the end of the line

H  Three lines of two rows of Chain stitch with one row of Buttonhole stitch worked over, in purple, pink/gold and green/gold

I  Five lines of Chain stitch crossed, each line with two rows of Chain stitch in green, pink, orange and purple. Bows are sewn at the ends of lines

J  Two curved lines of three rows of Chain stitch, edged with Buttonhole stitch, in blue and orange

K  Lines of Chain stitch with rows twisted over each other in pink, green/gold and mauve

L  Lines of two rows of Chain stitch crossed in pink, blue and purple

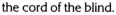
# Jane's window

This embroidered picture is worked with a combination of fabric dye crayons and free surface stitchery. Several stitches have been used to give the various effects – leaves, flowers, brickwork and louvred window shutters – and this type of picture presents an opportunity for trying out all the stitches you have learned so far in this book.

Perhaps it will give you ideas for your own embroidery design of a 'portrait' of your house or apartment.

## Materials required
38 × 75cm (15 × 30in) piece of white cotton fabric
Wooden frame approximately 35cm (14in) square.
Madeira stranded embroidery floss as follows: 1 skein each of M3328 russet pink, M352 salmon, M351 orange, M602 bright pink, M798 mid-blue, M906 bright green, M955 pale jade, M913 mid-jade, M943 emerald, M911 bright jade
Crewel needle, size 7
1 packet of fabric dye crayons
Piece of cardboard 28 × 31cm (11 × 12½in)
Fine string or buttonhole thread
A large sheet of tracing paper

## Preparation
Fold the fabric in half to give a stronger and firmer double layer measuring 38cm (15in) square.

Place the tracing paper over the picture on this page and trace it, using the fabric dye crayons to draw and colour in the window and brickwork design. Take care not to smudge the waxy crayons, as this will give a blurred effect on the finished fabric.

Transfer the tracing onto the doubled fabric, following the manufacturer's instructions.

Stretch the doubled fabric over the frame.

## Working the embroidery
The brickwork lines are embroidered in three strands of M3328 in rows of Running stitch. The shaded bricks are then worked over in several Cross stitches using three strands of M352.

The bright pink and red geraniums (M351 and M602) are worked with six strands of thread in small clusters of

Detached Chain stitch which are placed very closely together so that they give a rich and massed effect.

The small blue flowers (M798) are worked in six strands of thread and are formed by working two or three French knots for each flower to give a richly raised effect.

The small salmon-coloured flowers are similarly worked in six strands as tiny Cross stitches, using M352.

The window shutters are worked in six strands of mid-jade (M913). The louvre pattern is created by working lines of Blanket stitch across each shutter which is then outlined in Back stitch.

Back stitch, in three strands of thread (M955), is also used to outline the upper half of the window, which appears as a pale green blind, and then similarly in darker green (M913) for the lower half of the window.

Using this same green thread, work a scalloped line of Blanket stitch across the lower edge of the window blind, varying the size of the Blanket stitches to create the scallop shapes. From the centre point of this edge, work a short line of Chain stitches and then a small circlet of Blanket stitches to represent the cord of the blind.

The same green thread is also used to work the tiny Straight stitch stalks of the flowers which decorate the blind.

Work the flowers of the blind in M352, using six strands together, working three small Straight stitches radiating outwards from each stalk.

Work the stems of the geraniums in M906, using six strands together and working small, even Back stitches.

Similarly, work the grassy leaves in M911 in curved lines of Back stitches to give a spiked effect.

The geranium leaves are worked with three strands of thread, using M943 and M911 as appropriate, working circles of Blanket stitch to give the full and rounded shapes that are required.

Finally, the sprigs of tiny leaves are worked by building up small groups of Detached Chain stitches in M906 and M943, encircling the blue and salmon flowers and then trailing downwards so that they appear to be growing from the window box.

When the stitchery is complete, remove the fabric from the frame. Stretch the fabric, lacing it over the card. The picture is now ready for framing.

# House 'portrait'

Whether you live in a small, individual town house, a country cottage, a house in a row or in an apartment, you can probably work a charming 'portrait' of your home in embroidery. Take a photograph as straight-on as you can and have it enlarged to a workable size. Trace and re-trace the picture, simplifying fussy details and perhaps even removing unsightly features, such as down pipes. Emphasise those features which you think give your home character – perhaps an unusual window shape, or decorative roof details. When the design seems pleasing, trace it onto fabric and colour with crayons before planning the embroidery.

## Working the embroidery

If you are using a new shirt, wash it first so that it does not shrink later and pucker your stitches.

If possible, mount the area to be worked on a ring frame. Thread the needle with three strands of the cotton. Don't knot it, but begin with some tiny neat back stitches which you will then cover up with your embroidery.

Work the cornflowers in straight rows of chain stitch sewn from the centre outwards. The poppy is worked in chain stitch filling, with the flower outlined and then filled in.

Next work the yellow corn in detached chain stitch and make your straight catching stitches long enough to look like the whiskers on the ears of corn. Use detached chain stitch again to work the black centre of the poppy. Then sew the bright green grass in stem stitch and the darker green stems in back stitch. The poppy bud is worked in green chain stitch and red straight stitches. At the lower edge of the design, extend your stitches 6mm (¼in) inside the pocket.

## Finishing

Finish threads off by working a few small stitches in the back of the work and snipping off. Make sure the wrong side is neat and that you have not carried thread across white areas where it will show through on the right side.

*Use the trace design below for the flowers on the shirt above. Transfer it using one of the methods already described.*

# A pocketful of flowers

Breathe new life into a plain shirt with this fresh and pretty design of cornfield flowers. Work the motif in basic stitches on to a white or plain-coloured shirt with a breast pocket from which the flowers will appear to spring.

## Materials required

Coats Anchor stranded cotton as follows: 1 skein each of 0238 and 0267 green, 046 red, 0132 blue, 0305 yellow and 0403 black
Crewel needle, size 8 or 9
Tracing paper and tacking thread or dressmaker's carbon paper
Small ring frame if possible

# Amusing motifs for children's clothes

These brightly coloured mice make fun motifs to use on a party dress, T shirt or top and skirt. You do not have to use the colours given here – vary them according to the type of garment you are embroidering.

Work the motif on a stretch fabric using a Vilene backing to hold it in shape, or on any suitable lightweight fabric.

## Materials required

Coats Anchor stranded cotton as
    follows: 1 skein each of 0255 green,
    0291 yellow, 316 tangerine, 0403
    black and 0410 turquoise
Crewel needle, size 7
Lightweight iron-on Vilene (for stretch
    fabrics only)
Dressmaker's carbon paper
Child's dress or skirt and top

## Working the embroidery

In the photograph, the complete design is used for the top, and the left-hand mouse only, for the skirt.

Trace the motif on to a sheet of paper and place in the desired position on garment. Transfer on to the fabric using dressmaker's carbon paper.

If your garment is made from a stretch fabric, cut a small piece of lightweight, iron-on Vilene and apply this to the wrong side of the fabric, immediately behind the design. This will prevent the fabric from stretching while you are working the embroidery.

Use the key as a guide to stitches to use. For the colour schemes, see the photograph above.

When the embroidery is complete, press on the wrong side.

*Right: There are two colour schemes for the motif. Use either one for the single mouse on the skirt.*

Trace pattern

tail and whiskers = back stitch

flower centres and eyes = detached chain

petals and noses = chain stitch

outline of body = stem stitch

# Ribbon Embroidery

One of the oldest ribboncraft techniques recorded is that of ribbon embroidery.
Traditionally, ribbon embroidery is couched, flowers and leaves being formed by
folding and pleating ribbons and catching down the edges. Modern ribbon
embroidery introduces the use of simple surface stitches.
Ribbon embroidery is essentially a freestyle form of decoration. The general
outline of the design is indicated on the fabric with basting stitches or chalk
pencil, and the work is carried out according to the creativity of the embroiderer.

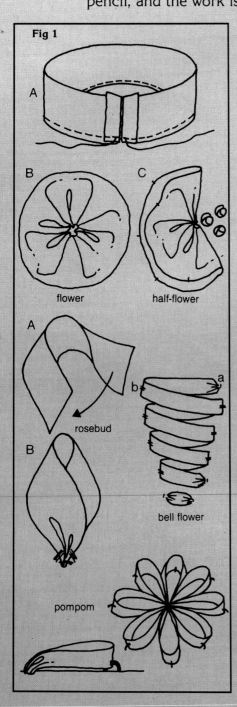

Fig 1

A

B     C

flower     half-flower

A

rosebud

b

a

B

bell flower

pompom

## Victorian posy

The framed embroidery is worked on
an oval shape 20×16cm *(8×6½in)*.

### Materials required
30×26cm *(12×10¼in)* pink fabric
1m *(1⅛yd)* double face polyester
    satin ribbons of each of the
    following: 1.5mm *(1/16 in)*-wide Light
    Pink 117, Pink 150, Dusty Rose
    160, Persimmon 240, Willow 563;
    3mm *(⅛in)*-wide Rosy Mauve 165,
    Rose Pink 154, Willow 563; 10mm
    *(⅜in)*-wide Light Pink 117
1m *(1⅛yd)* of 10mm *(⅜in)*-wide
    Feather-edge satin ribbon in Peach
    720, Light Pink 117
Anchor stranded embroidery threads
    in Cream 0386, Moss 0264,
    Geranium 541, Rose 048
Small crystal beads
Card, pelmet-weight interfacing, clear
    adhesive
Tapestry needle, embroidery needle

### Working the design
To catch down the different kinds of
ribbon flowers, use tiny, single

stitches, which should be hidden
under the ribbons. Always start with
a back stitch on the wrong side and
finish off stitches on the wrong side.
Stitches may be worked from one
ribbon flower to the next.

Using two strands of embroidery
thread in the needle for stitching,
work from the picture, adapting the
placing of the various flowers, etc, to
please your own sense of design.
Remember that this is a freestyle
technique and your own ideas should
be expressed.

In ribbon embroidery, ribbon ends
are caught to the back of the work
with small hand-sewing stitches.
Work with about 45cm *(18in)* of
ribbon in the needle for surface
stitches. If the ribbon twists, drop the
needle and allow the ribbon to
untwist.

Fig 1 illustrates a few of the
shapes that can be achieved with
ribbon. Surface stitches in Victorian
Posy include Detached Chain, Open
Chain and French Knots, some
worked in narrow ribbons, some in
stranded threads.

### Finishing
Do not press ribbon embroidery. Cut
card into shape to fit a frame. Cut
stiff interfacing to the same shape
and size. Lay the embroidery wrong
side up and place the card on top.
Pencil round lightly and trim the
fabric back to 4cm *(1½in)* from the
pencilled line. Lay embroidery wrong
side up again and place interfacing,
then card, on top. Bring the edges of
the fabric on to the card and glue
down, pulling the fabric smooth and
ensuring that there are no creases or
pleats on the right side of the work.
Leave to dry, then place in a frame.

**Fig 1** *Flower:* join cut ends of ribbon and
*gather one edge (A). Draw up into a rosette (B)*
***Half-flower:*** *fold flower and couch down
centre. Add a few French Knots (C)*
***Rosebud:*** *fold ribbon (A) and join cut ends,
gathering and stitching down (B)*
***Bell flower:*** *bring ribbon through fabric at (a).
Fold and catch it down at (b). Continue folding
and catching down to make a bell shape. Take
end back through fabric*
***Pompom:*** *fold and stitch ribbon into loops and
catch down on selvedge edges of loops*

Designed by Mary Pilcher

# Summer daisies

Narrow ribbons can be used in place of conventional embroidery threads if the design and stitches are simple. The Summer Daisies design uses only three stitches: French Knots, Open Fishbone, and Lazy Daisy worked so that the point of the stitch lies on the outside edge of the finished flower.

### Materials required
*Finished size 43cm (17in) diameter*
1.10m *(1¼yd)* of 114cm *(45in)*-wide
   blue polyester satin fabric
Matching Drima sewing thread
3.60m *(4yd)* piping cord
1.5mm *(¹⁄₁₆ in)*-wide double face
   polyester satin ribbons as follows:
   5m *(5½yd)* Mint 530; 3m *(3¼yd)*
   Light Pink 117, Light Orchid 430,
   Light Blue 305; 3.50m *(3⅞yd)* Iris
   447
Tissue paper, basting thread, needle

### Preparation
From the fabric, cut a circle 30cm *(12in)* diameter for the embroidery. For the cushion cut two circles 45cm *(18in)* diameter. From one circle cut a round hole in the middle 19cm *(7½in)* diameter. From the remaining blue fabric cut and join 10cm *(4in)*-wide strips to make a 1.45m *(1⅝yd)* length for the gusset. Cut bias strips 2.5cm *(1in)* wide to cover the piping cord. Cut the cord into two pieces, 1.45m *(1⅝yd)* and 67cm *(26½in)* long, and cover with bias strips.
   Place the 30cm *(12in)* fabric circle in an embroidery frame. Trace the lines of the design from the facing page on to tissue paper. Baste tissue to the fabric.

### Working the design
Work embroidery through the tissue paper and follow the picture for colours and stitches.
   Stems are ribbon couched down with ribbon (Fig 1). Petals and leaves are worked in reversed Lazy Daisy stitches (Fig 2). French Knots are worked for flower centres and Open Fishbone for grass heads.
   When embroidery is completed, gently tear away the tissue and remove embroidery from the frame.

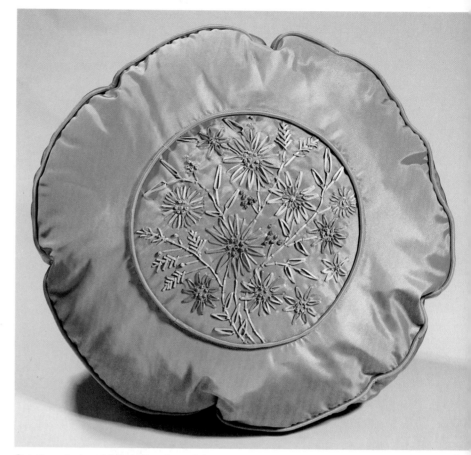

Cut the circle of fabric back to 24cm *(9½in)* in diameter.

### Making up the cushion
On the cushion piece with the hole, pin, baste and machine-stitch the covered piping round the hole edge on the right side, cut edge of fabric to cut edge. Press seam allowance to the wrong side. Place the embroidery underneath and baste in place. Stitch from the wrong side, working stitches along previous row of piping stitching.
   Pin, baste and stitch piping round the outside edge of the same cushion piece. Pin, baste and stitch piping round the edge of the second cushion piece on the right side.
   Pin the short ends of the gusset piece and check that it fits round the cushion. Baste and stitch short ends. Pin, baste and stitch the gusset to the top cushion piece, right sides facing. Work the second cushion piece to the gusset in the same way, leaving a 25cm *(10in)* gap in the seam for inserting the cushion pad. Close seam with hand-sewing.

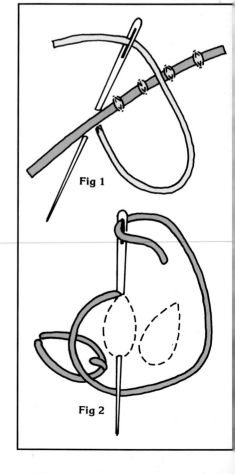

Fig 1

Fig 2

**Fig 1** *Couching for stems*

**Fig 2** *Reversed Lazy Daisy for petals and leaves*

*Delicate summer colours in ribbon embroidery worked on polyester satin make a pretty cushion. Above, the panel is reproduced life-size for you to trace*

# Little town

In traditional ribbon embroidery, techniques tend to produce flower and foliage effects. Here is an example of modern ribbon embroidery where narrow ribbons have been couched down on fabric in rows to produce solid areas of colour. In some places, Straight stitches have been used for couching; in others, Cross stitches produce a more textured effect. Other decorative surface embroidery stitches may be used to couch ribbons for an even greater variety of effects.

The stitch guide and key are shown overleaf.

## Materials required

*Finished size 24×26cm (9½×10¼in)*
50×56cm *(20×22in)* cream evenweave linen or similar fabric
24×26cm *(9½×10¼in)* stitch-and-
   tear embroidery backing material
1.5mm *(¹⁄₁₆in)*-wide double face
   polyester satin ribbons as follows:
   7.50m *(8¼yd)* Light Blue 305; 6m
   *(6⅝yd)* Silver 012, Pink 150;
   4.50m *(5yd)* White 029; 3.50m
   *(3⅞yd)* Baby Maize 617; 2.50m
   *(2¾yd)* Red 250, Emerald 580,
   Tan 835; 2m *(2¼yd)* Sable 843,
   Capri Blue 337; 1.60m *(1¾yd)*
   Persimmon 240, Peach 720,
   Strawberry 157, Hot Pink 156,
   Sienna 770; 1m *(1⅛yd)* Lemon
   640, Turftan 847, Rosewood 169,
   Willow 563, Light Orchid 430
Anchor stranded embroidery threads
   as follows: 1 skein of Emerald
   0227, Terra Cotta 0336, Grey
   0397; oddments of Forest Green
   0218, Grass Green 0242, Peat
   0360, Beige 0379, Terra Cotta
   0341, Nasturtium 0328, Cobalt
   Blue 0131, 0128, Kingfisher 0160,
   Canary 0288, Gorse 0300,
   Blossom Pink 038, Rose 048, Old
   Rose 076, Red 047, White 0402,
   Black 0403
Tissue paper, basting thread, needle
Matching Drima sewing threads

## Preparation

Trace your pattern from the stitch guide overleaf. Use a ruler to outline the houses, then draw in the flowers, trees, path, flower beds, clock face and round-topped doors, etc.

Press all creases from the fabric.

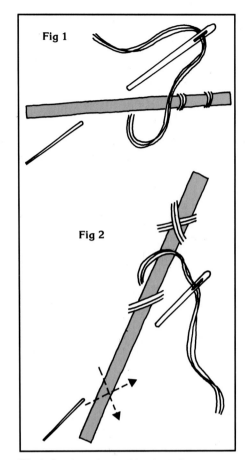

**Fig 1** *Couching down ribbon with Straight stitches in embroidery thread*

**Fig 2** *Couching down ribbon with Cross stitches in embroidery thread*

Mark the centre of the fabric with threads and then measure and mark the working area 24×26cm *(9½×10¼in)* from the centre, in threads. Baste the stitch-and-tear material to the back of the fabric on the working area. Pin the traced pattern to the fabric and work small running stitches along all the pattern lines. When completed, gently tear away the tissue paper. Put the fabric in an embroidery frame.

## Basic techniques for working with ribbons and threads

1. Cut ribbons into approximately 45cm *(18in)* lengths. Use three strands of embroidery threads together throughout the work. Follow the stitch guide overleaf for the direction of couching and as a guide to the use of Straight stitch and Cross stitch.
2. Thread a length of ribbon into a large-eyed but sharp needle and

*Designed by Linda Wood*

bring it through from the wrong side of the fabric, leaving about 2cm (¾in) at the back. Catch down the end with a few hand-sewing stitches.

3. To couch with Straight stitches, see Fig 1, page 78. Bring the embroidery thread through from the wrong side and, laying the ribbon with the thumb, make the first stitch to hold the ribbon in position, taking the needle through to the wrong side. Bring the needle through again a short distance away (see Fig 1) for the second couching stitch.

4. To couch with Cross stitches, see Fig 2, page 78.

5. When you reach the end of the first row of couching take the ribbon on its needle under three or four threads of fabric and bring it through to the front again ready for the second row. As you can see from the picture of the Little Town on the previous page, couching stitches are alternated between those of the previous row, to simulate bricks or roof tiles.

6. To finish a length of ribbon, take the end through to the wrong side and secure with hand-sewing stitches.

7. Complete all the ribbon work first, then work the freestyle decorative embroidery using stranded threads. Do not press ribbonwork because it spoils the effect.

## Working the design

The stitch guide shows the direction in which the ribbon is laid and where Straight stitches and Cross stitches are used for couching. The key below identifies ribbon colours and embroidery threads for each area of the picture. Refer to the picture on the previous page for the embroidery stitches used for flowers, foliage, sky, path, etc.

Work paths, lawns and sky in Seeding. Flowers are worked in French knots, Open Chain stitch, Straight stitch and Lazy Daisy. Outline windows and doors in Stem stitch. The church door looks very effective outlined with a flat plait (see Fig 1, page 111) of Silver 012 ribbon. Use stranded threads for smaller leaves, branches and flower stems.

*Right, stitch guide for the Little Town picture on the previous page, showing directional working for couching down ribbons*

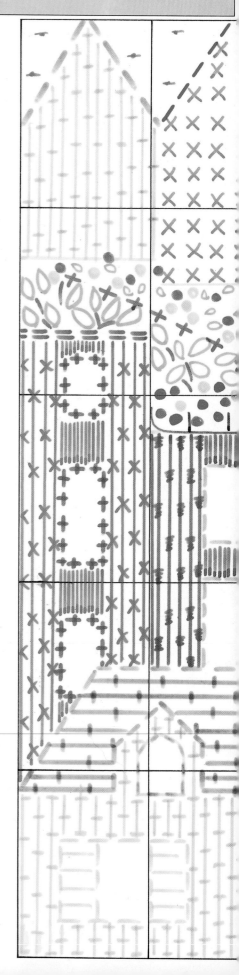

## Key to stitch guide

| Ribbons | (couched with) Threads |
|---|---|
| Silver 012 | Grey 0397 |
| White 029 | Grey 0397 |
| White 029 | White 0402 |
| Baby Maize 617 | Gorse 0300 |
| Peach 720 | Peat 0360 |
| Persimmon 240 | Nasturtium 0328 |
| Pink 150 | Rose 048 |
| Rosewood 169 | Old Rose 076 |
| Light Blue 305 | Kingfisher 0160 |
| Capri Blue 337 | Cobalt Blue 0131 |
| Sable 843 | Beige 0379 |
| Turftan 847 | Peat 0360 |
| Tan 835 | Peat 0360 |
| Sienna 770 | |
| Light Blue 305 | |
| Silver 012 | |

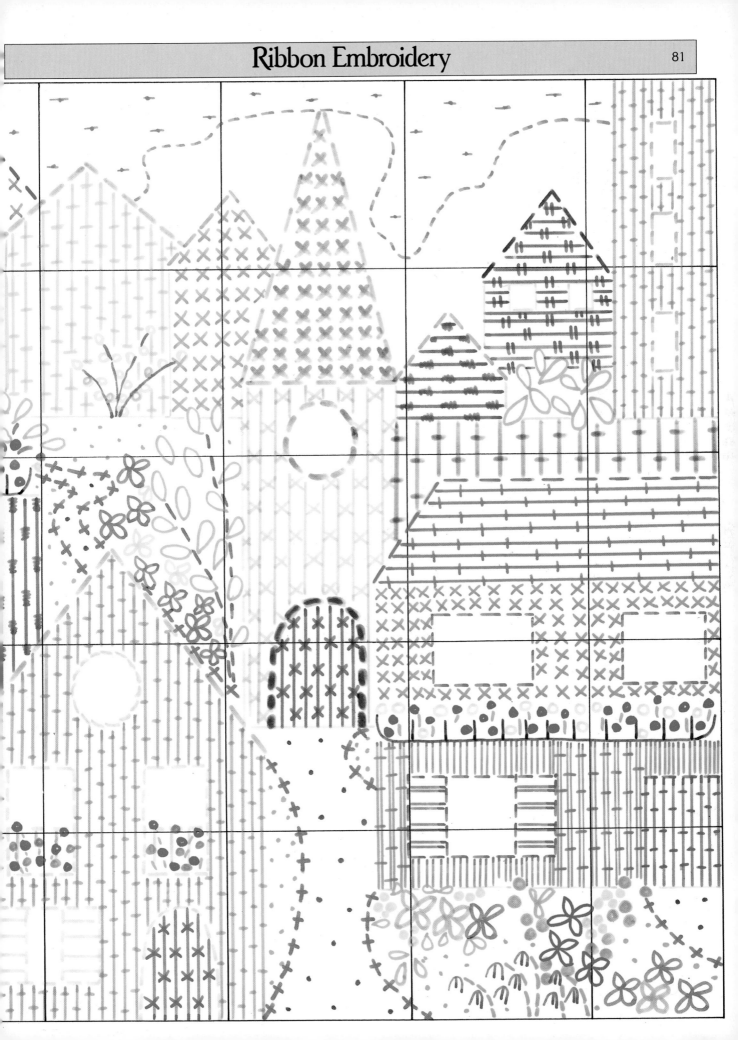

# Hanging planter

The pretty planter is made of plastic canvas embroidered with ribbons. Florentine or Bargello stitch has been used here but any straight stitch with a similar effect could be used. Plastic canvas, a comparatively new embroidery material, is useful when a strong structure is being worked, such as a picture frame or a box. Plastic canvas is also ideal for making church kneelers, book covers, purses and bags – as well as fashion accessories and soft jewellery.

Ribbons work well on this material used either with tapisserie yarns for textural interest or, as on the planter, when a hard-wearing finish is required. As polyester ribbons are washable and colourfast, the embroidered planter can be washed if it becomes soiled and the colours will not fade in strong sunlight.

## Materials required
*Finished size 12.5×11.5cm (5×4½in)*
Sheet of plastic canvas 7 holes to 2.5cm *(1in)*
3mm *(⅛in)*-wide double face polyester satin ribbons as follows: 8.25m *(9yd)* Indian Orange 756; 8.25m *(9yd)* Yellow Gold 660; 33m *(36yd)* Cream 815
2.50m *(2¾yd)* white cotton furnishing cord and a tassel
2 pieces of 11.5cm *(4½in)* square stiff card
Tapestry needle, hand-sewing needle
White Drima sewing thread

## Preparation
Cut four pieces of plastic canvas 12.5×11.5cm *(5×4½in)* for the sides of the planter, making sure that the edges are cut smooth.

Cut a piece of plastic canvas 11.5cm *(4½in)* square for the planter base.

## Working the design
Follow the picture as a guide to ribbon colours and the chart (Fig 1) for the stitchery, which shows one repeat. Each panel is worked with two and a half repeats, making five 'flame' points.

The chart shows the sequence of stitches from the foundation in

Indian Orange to the completion of the rows in Yellow Gold. When you have worked the last row of Yellow Gold the stitchery continues with Cream ribbon over four threads of canvas.

Row 1: Using Indian Orange ribbon in the needle and starting at the left, work the first stitch over two threads of canvas, the next stitch over four, then alternate over two, over four to the end of the row. The last stitch, on the right, is over four threads.

Row 2: In this row, the 'flame' points are established, which will enable you to work the remainder of the Florentine pattern. Still using Indian Orange ribbon and working from right to left, make the first stitch over the last but one stitch of the previous row and over four threads of canvas. Work two more stitches and you will see that you have completed your first 'flame' point. Now miss the next three stitches of the previous row and begin the second flame point on the fourth stitch. Continue in the same way right across the row, stepping stitches up and down in a zigzag pattern.

Row 3: Change to the Yellow Gold ribbon. You now have the basis of the pattern in Indian Orange to follow. Work from left to right and over four threads of canvas, placing each stitch immediately over each of the Indian Orange stitches.

Row 4: Work from right to left in Yellow Gold as you did for row 3.

Change to Cream ribbon and work the panel until you are within five threads of the edge. Complete the panel by working in Cream over five and three threads alternately.

Work all four side panels of the planter in the same way.

## Working the base
Use Cream ribbon throughout for the base. Work the first row exactly as for the sides, then continue working over four threads of canvas. The last row is worked over six and four threads alternately.

## Finishing
Using Cream ribbon, oversew one side piece to the base piece, working from the right side and working each stitch through one hole of canvas on the edges. Sew the second side piece

to the base, then the third and finally the fourth. Now work oversewing stitches to join the corners of the planter, still working from the right side.

Press the two pieces of stiff card into the base of the planter. Work oversewing stitches with Cream ribbon all round the top edge of the planter. To neaten the inside, hand-sew a small white plastic bag just inside the top edge, taking small stitches through the plastic canvas.

## Hanging the planter
Cut the cotton cord into two pieces. Wind cotton round the cut ends and sew to prevent the cord fraying. Pin the cord on to the bottom of the planter in a cross and then take the four ends up the side seams. Stitch the cord to the planter with hand-sewing stitches and thread. Knot the four ends at the top for hanging. (Slip a large brass ring on to the knot if preferred.) Sew the tassel underneath the planter.

**Fig 1** *Stitch chart for the Hanging Planter, showing one repeat and the sequence of stitches from the foundation in Indian Orange to the completion of the rows in Yellow Gold*

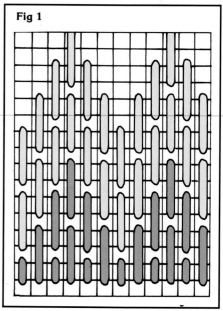

Fig 1

## Hints on working ribbons on plastic canvas

Do not knot the ribbon end when starting embroidery. Hold the end down on the wrong side with your thumb and work the first two or three stitches over the end to secure it. When finishing a length of ribbon, work the end under previous stitches.

Ribbon tends to twist while working but this can be minimised if you hold the ribbon smooth and flat along the canvas as you make each stitch. Slip the needle through, holding the ribbon down firmly on the canvas with the thumb. Pull the ribbon through and the stitch will remain smooth on the right side. Do the same as you prepare to bring the ribbon back through from the wrong side. Hold the ribbon smoothly with the fingers against the canvas on the wrong side and as you bring the needle through, keep your fingers in position, holding the ribbon.

You will get a little twisting even using this technique but small twists are easily removed with the needle point. If the ribbon should twist excessively, drop the needle and allow the ribbon to untwist naturally.

## More ideas for plastic canvas

Plastic canvas can also be obtained in a finer mesh of 10 holes to 2.5cm (1in), and 1.5mm (1/16 in)-wide ribbon can be used on this. This finer-mesh plastic canvas is ideal for making bracelets, hairbands, bookmarks and soft jewellery. Bracelets are made with plastic canvas strips 25cm (10in) long by 2.5cm (1in) wide. Leave 12mm (1/2in) unworked at one end and overlap the ends. Embroider and oversew edges to finish through both thicknesses of canvas.

Hairbands worked in ribbons on plastic canvas look pretty and fashionable. Cut plastic canvas to about the same length as for bracelets but a little wider. Leave two holes of plastic canvas unworked at the ends, snip the plastic threads with scissors and slip elastic through the holes to fasten the hairband.

For bookmarks, which make very pretty gifts, embroider strips of fine-mesh plastic canvas, and soft jewellery, such as brooches, earrings and pendants, is particularly effective worked with Lurex ribbons.

# Candlewicking with ribbon

Candlewicking is a traditional American craft dating back to pioneer days when women used the linen yarn intended for candle wicks to embroider coarse, unbleached linen, in an attempt to make their home furnishings more attractive. The same simple stitches, worked in narrow, cream ribbons on natural-coloured fabrics, are a modern interpretation of an old and charming craft.

## Butterfly motif

The butterfly design is worked on even-weave cotton and, on this fabric, could be mounted and framed for a wall picture. As the butterfly is such a versatile motif, however, it could also be worked as a decoration for fashion accessories or home furnishings (see illustrations).

**Fig 1** *Trace the butterfly, then reverse the tracing to obtain the whole motif*

## Materials required

*Finished motif size 11 × 20cm (4½ × 8in)*
12m *(13¼yd)* of 1.5mm *(¹⁄₁₆ in)*-wide Cream 815 double face polyester satin ribbon
40×33cm *(16×13in)* unbleached cotton fabric
1 ball of Pearl cotton, Ecru No. 5
Tissue paper, basting thread, needle

## Preparation

Trace the butterfly motif from Fig 1 and reverse the tracing to obtain the whole motif. Put the fabric into an embroidery frame. Baste the tracing to the fabric, or use dressmakers' carbon paper.

## Working the design

Work stitches through the tissue paper, if you are using this technique, tearing the paper away when embroidery is completed.
Work the design as follows:
**Head and tail:** Straight Satin stitch in ribbon.
**Body of butterfly:** Slanting Satin stitch in Pearl cotton, outlined with Stem stitch in Pearl cotton.
**Antenna and oval shapes on the wings:** Palestrina stitch (Fig 2) in Pearl cotton.
**Black dots:** Colonial Knots (Fig 3) in ribbon.
**Crosses:** Colonial Knots in Pearl cotton.
**Flower petals:** Lazy Daisy stitches in ribbon first, then work a second petal on top in Pearl cotton.

## Finishing

It is advisable not to press ribbon embroidery but if it is really necessary, press lightly with the embroidery face down on a towel.

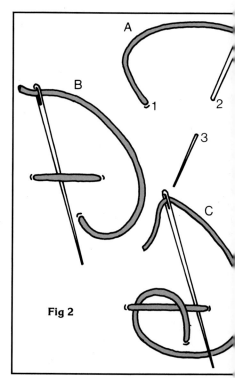

**Fig 2** *Palestrina stitch: this is worked from left to right. Bring needle up through fabric (A1). Make a stitch to the right about 6mm (¼in) away (A2) and come up through the fabric about 3mm (⅛in) below and slightly to the left (A3). Pull the thread through, then go back over and under the straight stitch (B). Without tightening the thread, again go under the straight stitch (C). Now pull the thread through gently to form the stitch. Make the next stitch to the right by inserting the needle 6mm (¼in) away, as A1-2*

**Fig 3** *Colonial Knot: bring needle through to right side of fabric at A1 and swing thread around needle in a clockwise loop. Wrap the thread anticlockwise around the needle in a figure-of-eight (B). Pull thread around needle gently and reinsert the needle a few threads away from the point the stitch was first started (Fig A1). Pull thread through fabric to make the Colonial Knot. Bring thread up through fabric again to the right side to make the next Knot*

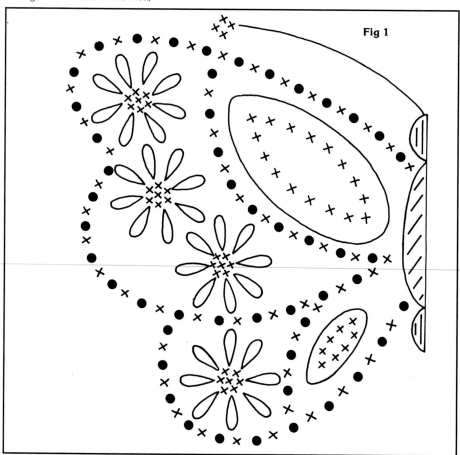

Fig 1

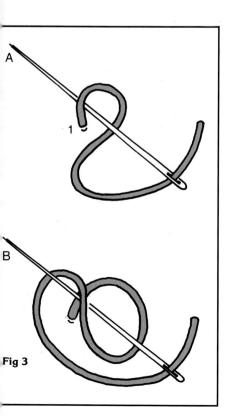

*Above, the butterfly motif is 11×20cm (4½×8in) and is worked here on cream even-weave cotton for a mounted and framed picture*

A

1

B

**Fig 3**

# Ideas for the butterfly motif

Candlewicking, using a few simple stitches, Pearl cotton and narrow ribbon, can be used to decorate all kinds of home furnishings and accessories. Use the butterfly motif for a cushion or pillow, working in white on a pastel-coloured fabric and edging the cushion with broderie anglaise (eyelet). Or work butterflies along the hem of curtains for a pretty bedroom scheme, with perhaps a single butterfly worked on a runner.

For personal items, the butterfly might be embroidered on even-weave linen for a wooden-handled work bag or, for a charming fashion look, on the back of a casual summer linen jacket.

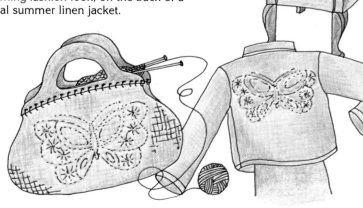

# Smocking

Smocking with fine ribbon lends a whole new dimension to the needlecraft. Bold and colourful effects can be achieved and fabrics such as furnishing cottons and wools can be worked. This means that ribbon smocking can be used not only for dresses, shirts, aprons and so on, but also for furnishings for the home.

## Fabrics for smocking

Suitable fabrics for ribbon smocking are cotton and cotton mixes, linen-type fabrics, fine wools and some furnishing fabrics. Very thick fabrics do not look so well when smocked. Traditionally, transfers of smocking dots are used as a guide to gathering the pleats, but if you are using fabric with a recognisable repeat or overall pattern, such as spots or gingham checks, you can dispense with the transfer and use the pattern itself as your guide.

Smocking reduces fabric to one-third of its original width and you should allow for this when measuring and buying fabric.

## Stitches in smocking

Three stitches only are all you need for ribbon smocking. Stem stitch, sometimes called Outline stitch (Fig 1), is used for firm control of gathers and is thus used at the top of a smocked band. Cable stitch (Fig 2) is used for medium control. Surface Honeycomb (Figs 3A and B) is a looser control stitch and, used at the bottom of a band, will release the fullness. The curtain heading in the picture is worked entirely in rows of Surface Honeycomb.

## Smocked curtains

### Materials required

*For a pair of curtains with a finished hem width of 152cm (60in) × 91cm (36in) long*
3.50m *(4yd)* of 120cm *(48in)*-wide printed cotton fabric
4m *(4½yd)* of 1.5mm *(¹⁄₁₆in)*-wide Red 250 double face polyester satin ribbon
Curtain hooks or rings as required
Drima sewing thread, needle

## Preparation

Cut and seam the fabric to make two pieces 155cm *(61in)* wide by 107cm *(42in)* long. Press seams open and neaten edges.

Turn the top edge of curtain over 5cm *(2in)* and press. The first row of gathering stitches is worked through the doubled fabric, 4cm *(1½in)* from the top edge. Work six rows of gathering stitches from side edge to side edge, the rows 15mm *(⅝in)* apart. Gathering stitches should also be about 15mm *(⅝in)* apart for this project. (They can be as close as 6mm *(¼in)*, depending on the fabric and the design.)

Pull up the six rows of gathering and twist the thread ends in pairs around pins (Fig 4). The width of the work should now be approximately 55cm *(22in)*. Adjust the pleats evenly. In smocking, the pleats are called 'reeds'.

Follow Figs 3A and B to work Surface Honeycomb, using ribbon in the needle. Ribbon ends should be fastened off on the wrong side of work for starting and finishing lengths; use small hand-stitches to catch ribbon to the fabric.

## Finishing

When all smocking has been completed, carefully withdraw the gathering threads. Do not press smocking.

To make up the curtains make narrow hems on both edges and machine-stitch. Press the hem fold to desired length. Machine-stitch a single narrow fold on the edge, then hand-sew the hem. Sew curtain hooks or rings to curtain head behind the smocking.

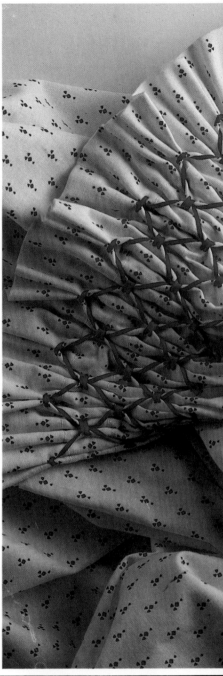

**Fig 1**

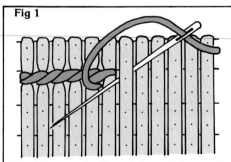

**Fig 1** *Stem or Outline stitch is a tight control stitch. Work from left to right along lines of gathering. Pick up one reed (pleat) with each stitch. Stem stitch can be varied by stepping stitches between rows to make patterns*

**Fig 2**

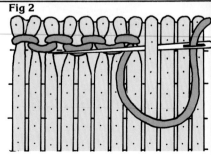

**Fig 2** *Cable stitch is a medium control stitch and each stitch joins two reeds. Work from left to right with the thread placed above and below the needle alternately. Several rows of Cable stitches can be worked close together*

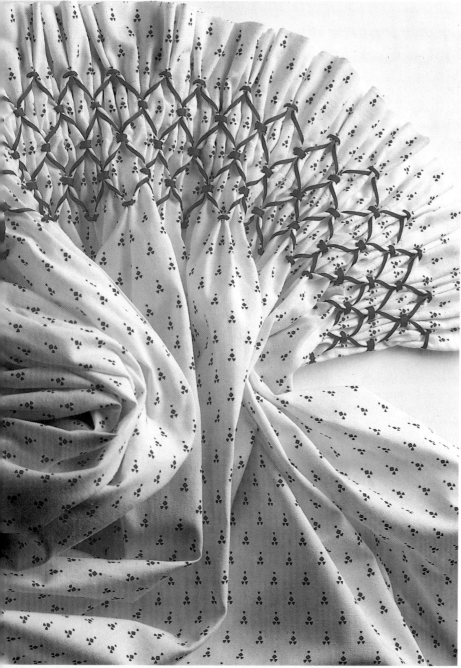

*Worked by Cathryn Brooker*

## Smocking ideas

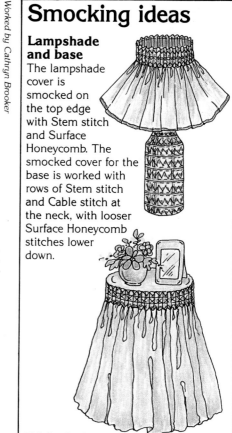

### Lampshade and base

The lampshade cover is smocked on the top edge with Stem stitch and Surface Honeycomb. The smocked cover for the base is worked with rows of Stem stitch and Cable stitch at the neck, with looser Surface Honeycomb stitches lower down.

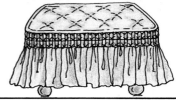

### Tablecloth

A circle of fabric is cut to fit the table top, then a straight length is smocked on the top edge to fit round the circle.

### Footstool

The top piece is quilted fabric, which is stitched to a straight piece of fabric smocked along the top edge to fit round the stool.

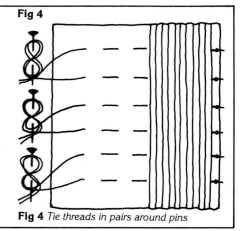

**Fig 3A**

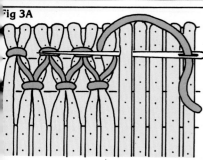

**Fig 3A** *Surface Honeycomb is worked over two rows of gathers. Take thread over two reeds in the top row and bring needle out at the side of the second reed. The thread lies on the surface while the needle moves down to the lower row*

**Fig 3B**

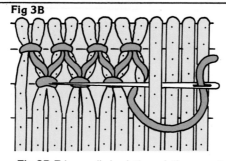

**Fig 3B** *Take needle back through the second reed in the lower row and then over to the third reed, pulling reeds two and three together. The thread then lies on the third reed while the needle moves up to the top row again*

**Fig 4**

**Fig 4** *Tie threads in pairs around pins*

# Embroidery on Lace

Lace is beautiful to look at and adds a touch of luxury wherever it is applied. In this chapter favourite needlework techniques — soft box-making, appliqué, beading, and embroidery on tulle and net — take on a new dimension when worked with lace.

Lace has always been used to enrich and embellish fabrics, whether for garments or furnishings. In past ages it has been used by the rich (both men and women) to show off their wealth, by wearing exquisitely hand-made lace collars, cuffs and dress trimmings. The finer and more intricate the lace, the wealthier the owner.

Often the lace would be lovingly re-used to decorate different garments, and family heirlooms such as christening robes would be transferred from one generation to another. Many different types of lace evolved — some were worked solely from thread, and for others the thread was worked on gossamer fine nets and cotton fabrics.

Today we are fortunate that with the advancement of modern machinery, techniques and man-made fibres, some of the beauty and finery of the priceless antique laces can be reproduced and is readily available to everyone. The following projects suggest to you some of the ways that modern commercially made lace can be used in conjunction with techniques such as hand and machine embroidery, appliqué and beading to produce a variety of beautiful items.

## LACECRAFT TECHNIQUES 1

### Joining lace end to end
Lengths of flat lace are joined by overlapping the ends and oversewing the edges. Match the pattern if possible for an almost invisible join. If lace is more than 2.5cm (1in) wide, turn the cut ends under before overlapping and sewing. Very wide laces, of 6.5–15cm (2½–6in), are best joined by cutting out round the pattern motif on both ends, and overlapping and stitching as for joining all-over lace (see Lacecraft Techniques 2, page 100).
**Note:** No. 50 machine embroidery cotton thread is recommended for all sewing with lace.

### Gathering lace edging
Pretty pre-gathered laces are widely available but they have a rather heavy heading, which can spoil the delicate effect when applied to lingerie or children's clothes. Lace edging, gathered by one of the methods described here, looks far prettier and is very simple to apply.
**Gathering by hand** Most hand-made and some machine-made lace edgings have a heavy thread running along the straight edge. Find this thread with a

needle-point and use it to pull up gathers. For a full ruffle, allow two and a half to three times the finished length.
**Gathering by machine** If the lace has no heavy thread, set the machine for a long stitch and loosen the top tension a little. Work two rows of stitching along the straight edge of wide lace edgings, and a single row of stitching for narrower, 12–25mm (½ – 1in), edgings. Pull up the gathers.

## Applying gathered lace to fabric

If the gathered lace is being applied to fabric as a surface ruffle (for instance, on the outline of a yoke), baste the lace in position and work a very fine zigzag stitch along the edge of the lace. Alternatively, straight stitching can be used but it is more likely to be visible.

To apply a gathered lace ruffle to the raw edge of fabric (such as for a fabric frill), work as follows:
1. Pin and baste the gathered lace along the edge of the fabric, right sides facing, with the lace heading about 6mm (¼in) from the fabric edge.
2. Set a zigzag stitch wide enough to catch the lace heading and go right off the edge of the fabric. The stitch will catch the raw fabric edge into the lace as you sew. Work the stitching slowly and stop every 5cm (2in) or so to

adjust the gathers you are about to sew.
3. Turn the work to the right side and press along the seam. Work a very narrow zigzag stitch along the seam from the right side (Fig 1).

## Making galloon ruffles

Galloon makes a very pretty ruffle as it has two decorative edges. It is a particularly effective trim for items that have a hemmed or finished edge (Fig 2).
1. Machine-gather the galloon lace about 9mm (⅜in) from one edge.
2. Pull up the gathers and stitch to the fabric with a straight stitch, working over the machine-gathering line.

## Whip stitching

Whip stitching is a useful technique for finishing the cut edges of lace or tulle and can also be used for hand-applying lace motifs to fabric or net.

Use No. 50 machine embroidery cotton thread or a pure silk thread, matching the colour closely.

Whip stitching is worked from right to left.
1. Do not tie a knot in the thread end. Instead, lay about 2.5cm (1in) of thread along the edge you are whipping and catch the end in as you sew.
2. As you near the end of the thread, cut off the end to about 2.5cm (1in) and lay the new thread alongside the old, whipping over both (Fig 3).

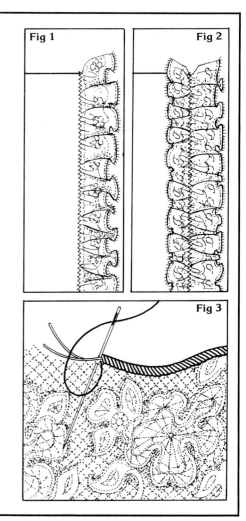

Fig 1 Fig 2 Fig 3

# Jewel box in lace

## Materials required

*Finished size 16 × 24 × 9.5cm*
*(6¼ × 9¼ × 3¾in)*
80 × 75cm *(31 × 30in)* soft plain fabric
80 × 75cm *(31 × 30in)* medium-weight
  interfacing
80 × 38cm *(31 × 15in)* all-over lace
1.40m *(1½yd)* of 5cm *(2in)*-wide lace
  edging
Sheet of thin card
All-purpose clear adhesive
Matching sewing threads
Matching stranded embroidery threads

## Preparation

Cut pieces of card as follows and mark
to identify them as instructed.
Two pieces of 16 × 24cm
*(6¼ × 9¼in)*. Mark on piece Top
Outer A, the other Bottom Outer B.
Two pieces 3mm *(⅛in)* smaller all
round. Mark one piece Top Lining a, the
other Bottom Lining b.
Two pieces 9.5 × 24cm *(3¾ × 9¼in)*.
Mark each Long Side Outer C.
Two pieces 3mm *(⅛in)* smaller all
round. Mark each Long Side Lining c.
Two pieces 9.5 × 16cm *(3¾ × 6¼in)*.
Mark each Short Side Outer D.
Two pieces 3mm *(⅛in)* smaller all
round. Mark each Short Side Lining d.
  Cut pieces of interfacing to the same
sizes plus 9mm *(⅜in)* all round. Cut
fabric to the same sizes plus 12mm
*(½in)* all round.
  Cut all-over lace for pieces A, B, C
and D (the outer box pieces) to the
same size as the fabric for these pieces.

## Working the design

Cover each piece of card with
interfacing, folding the edges over to
the other side and glueing them down.
Leave to dry under weights (books will
do).
  When dry, cover the interfacing with
the fabric pieces, folding the edges over
to the wrong side and glueing down.
Leave to dry under weights.
  Cover pieces A, B, C and D with the
all-over lace, mounting the lace over the
fabric side of the cards and glueing
down on the wrong side. Leave to dry.

## Assembling the box

Gather the lace edging with tiny
stitches. Neaten the cut ends of the lace
with oversewing. Sew the lace round the
box lid (piece A) on one long side and
two short sides, working on the wrong
side of the lid 3mm *(⅛in)* inside the
edge. Use hemming stitches. Press
gathers where stitched.
  Glue the lining pieces to the outer
pieces, card sides together. Centre the
lining pieces on the outers for all
sections of the box.
  Join the box pieces together with
hand-sewing. Using matching thread,
oversew the two long sides and the two
short sides to the box base, then sew
the box corners together.
  If you wish you can embellish your
jewel box with decorative stitching
along the edges; this will also neaten
them.
  Embroidery stitches such as Cretan,
Herringbone and Feather (see page 12)
can all be used to efficiently join the box
sides and decorate it at the same time.
However, you may wish to oversew the
sides together before working the
decorative stitching. Remember to
practise your stitching first to make sure
it gives the desired effect – you can
adjust the size of the stitch or even
choose a contrasting coloured thread.
  Oversew the lid to the back edge of
the box. If preferred, a loop and button
fastener can be sewn to the lid and the
box. Alternatively, sew ribbons to the lid
and the box and tie in a bow. Decorate
the box lid if required with beading (see
page 96) or embroidery.

# Lace appliqué cushions

Lace appliqué can produce different effects depending on the type of lace used and the techniques involved. The two cushions pictured use guipure and organdie motifs, chosen to make flower and leaf garlands. Some of the petals and leaves are left free of the background fabric, giving an extra dimension to the needlework.

Both cushions are made on the same basic design – a central hexagon of ribbons surrounding a circlet of flowers, with garlands of flowers and leaves grouped around the hexagon. Use washable fabrics to make the cushions and pre-shrink guipure and organdie motifs, so that the finished cushions can be home-laundered.

**Fig 1** *Pencil round the paper circle on the satin fabric square and mark the six points*

**Fig 2** *Baste and stitch the strips of ribbon round the marked circle*

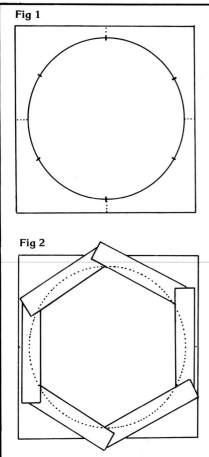

Fig 1

Fig 2

# White lace garland cushion

## Materials required
*Finished size (without ruffle) 38cm (15in) square*

50cm *(20in)* of 120cm *(48in)*-wide white polyester satin fabric

50cm *(20in)* of 120cm *(48in)*-wide white embroidered net fabric

4 large guipure or organdie motifs

8 each of three different guipure motifs

3.75m *(4⅛yd)* of 18mm *(¾in)*-wide white double face satin ribbon

1.60m *(1¾yd)* of 18mm *(¾in)*-wide white textured ribbon

2.50m *(2¾yd)* of 10cm *(4in)*-wide lace edging

Cushion pad

Pattern paper

Pair of compasses

## Preparation
Cut a 20cm *(8in)* square from the satin fabric and mark the middle by creasing both ways. Draw a circle on paper with a 9cm *(3½in)* radius. Using the compasses, mark six points on the circumference of the circle at regular intervals. Cut out the paper circle and pin it to the centre of the satin square. Pencil round the circle on the fabric and mark in the six points (Fig 1).

Cut six pieces of the textured ribbon 14cm *(5½in)* long and six pieces 11cm *(4½in)* long. Cut six pieces of satin ribbon 12.5cm *(5in)* long and four pieces 38cm *(15in)* long.

From the satin fabric cut two pieces 40cm *(16in)* square. Cut a piece of embroidered net to the same size. Join the ends of the lace

edging (see Lacecraft Techniques 1, page 88).

## Working the design

Baste the six shorter strips of textured ribbon round the marked circle on the satin square (Fig 2). Machine-stitch on the inner edge. Baste the six shorter strips of white satin ribbon next, overlapping the first row of ribbons by about half. Machine-stitch on the inner edge. Baste the remaining six textured ribbon strips in the same way, to form the third, outer row. Machine-stitch on both edges.

Pin and baste the net to the right side of one satin piece. Baste the four long strips of satin ribbon to the edges and then machine-stitch on the inside edge using a wide zigzag machine-stitch or any decorative machine embroidery stitch (page 148).

Hand-appliqué a circle of flower motifs to the centre of the hexagon.

Trim the satin square back to within 6mm (1/4in) of the hexagon edges. Turn the satin edge under, baste and then zigzag-stitch the hexagon to the middle of the net-covered cushion piece.

Arrange the lace motifs around the hexagon. Place the four large motifs at the corners and the rest in between, to create a natural flow of flowers and leaves. There need not be symmetry in the arrangement.

Hand-sew the motifs to the cushion piece, taking tiny stitches on the edges of the motifs and through the fabric background. Work some of the stitches inside the edges of the motifs so that the edges are slightly free of the background. Do not press the finished work.

## Finishing

Gather the lace edging for the cushion ruffle (see Lacecraft Techniques 1, page 88) and make up the cushion cover (see page 112).

Make small stitched bows from the remaining white satin ribbon and sew over 10cm (4in) fish-tailed ends at the corners (see picture).

# Tan and ecru cushion

Four different toning ribbons are used, as follows: 2.50m (2¾yd) white satin ribbon; 2.15m (2⅜yd) tan satin ribbon; 1.20m (1⅜yd) cream satin ribbon; 75cm (30in) cream textured ribbon.

The guipure and organdie motifs grouped in the hexagon centre and round the edges, on cream embroidered net fabric, are in a variety of tan shades, to tone with the ribbons.

## More ideas for lace appliqué

Lace appliqué, where a variety of motifs and shapes are sewn to a background fabric to make a design, lends itself to many uses in home furnishings and also to fashion. The sprays built up on the Tan and Ecru Cushion, for instance, would look superb worked on a satin bedspread. A single spray could be applied to the top of a soft jewellery box for a dressing-table accessory (Fig 1) and the same motif worked on a matching organdie runner.

For fashion work, a large area of applied lace and ribbons could be used on the back of an evening coat. Smaller appliquéd sprays or motifs could be sewn to the shoulder of a knitted sweater or cardigan.

Fig 1

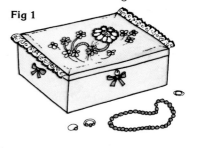

# Dream roses pillow

Shadow appliqué, lustrous satin ribbon and crisp broderie anglaise edging combine to make this charming pillow.

## Materials required
*Finished size (without ruffle)*
*28×34cm (11×13½in)*
40cm *(16in)* of 120cm *(48in)*-wide white cotton organdie
40cm *(16in)* of 120cm *(48in)*-wide white polycotton fabric for backing
2m *(2¼yd)* of 5cm *(2in)*-wide broderie anglaise edging
1.40m *(1½yd)* of 15mm *(⅝in)*-wide broderie anglaise beading
1.40m *(1½yd)* of 6mm *(¼in)*-wide double face satin ribbon
30cm *(12in)* squares cotton fabric for appliqué in red, dark, medium and light pinks, dark and light greens
6 pieces 30cm *(12in)* square lightweight iron-on interfacing
Stranded embroidery threads in dark, medium and light pinks, dark and light greens
Small amount of medium green tapestry wool
Cushion pad
Blunt-tipped needle, embroidery needle
Paste in solid stick form
Squared pattern paper, 1sq=2.5cm *(1in)*
Tracing paper

## Preparation
Draw the pattern (Fig 1) up to full size on squared pattern paper. Draw the outlines firmly. Trace off on to tracing paper to make the appliqué patterns.

From organdie cut a piece 31×37cm *(12×14½in)* for the embroidery. Cut a piece the same size from the cotton backing.

For the back of the pillow cut pieces of organdie and cotton to the same size as the front. Baste them together round the edges and then from corner to corner diagonally to hold the pieces firmly together during working.

Pin the backing fabric for the embroidery to the drawing on squared pattern paper. If the lines show through fairly clearly this will be sufficient guide for placing the appliqué pieces. If the lines are indistinct tape the pattern and fabric to a window and trace the pattern lines on to the fabric.

Iron the interfacing to the wrong side of the red, pink and green appliqué fabrics. Cut the tracing paper pattern into pieces and, following the graph pattern (Fig 1), use the pieces to cut shapes from the red, pink and green fabrics. No turnings are necessary. Tiny pieces, such as the centres of roses, are easier to cut freehand.

As pieces are cut, unpin the paper patterns and paste each in position on the cotton fabric, overlapping edges a little where shapes meet. Very small shapes are placed on top of larger pieces. Lay the organdie over the work, matching fabric edges. Baste the layers together round the outside edges.

## Working the design
Using two strands of thread in the embroidery needle, work running stitches round the shapes through both thicknesses of fabric, matching thread colours to fabrics.

When changing thread colours, knot the thread end and bring the needle through from the back. To finish thread ends, work a backstitch on the wrong side of work through the backing fabric.

Working from the picture, add petals to the roses and veins to the leaves. For the stems, work two rows of running stitches 3mm (⅛in) apart.

To complete the shadow appliqué, thread the blunt-tipped needle with green tapestry wool and, working on the wrong side of the work, push the needle through the backing fabric and thread the wool along the main stems. Leave about 12mm (½in) of wool hanging at beginning and end without knotting.

## Finishing

Join the ends of the broderie anglaise edging with a straight seam and press the seam open. Neaten the edges with zigzag stitch.

Gather the straight edge and fit the ruffle round the piece of embroidery, matching straight edges of ruffle and fabric. Pin and then baste. Machine-stitch the ruffle to the pillow piece. Remove basting threads.

Make up the pillow as for a cushion, inserting a zip into one of the side seams. Remove basting threads from the back.

Thread the ribbon through the broderie anglaise beading. Hand-sew the beading to the pillow, following the picture and neatly mitring the corners (see page 114 for technique). Tie the ends of the ribbon in a bow at one corner.

**Fig 1** *Graph pattern for Dream Roses shadow appliqué, 1sq = 2.5cm (1in)*

**Key to colours**
- □ red
- ○ light pink
- ✕ medium pink
- ■ dark pink
- ● light green
- ▲ dark green

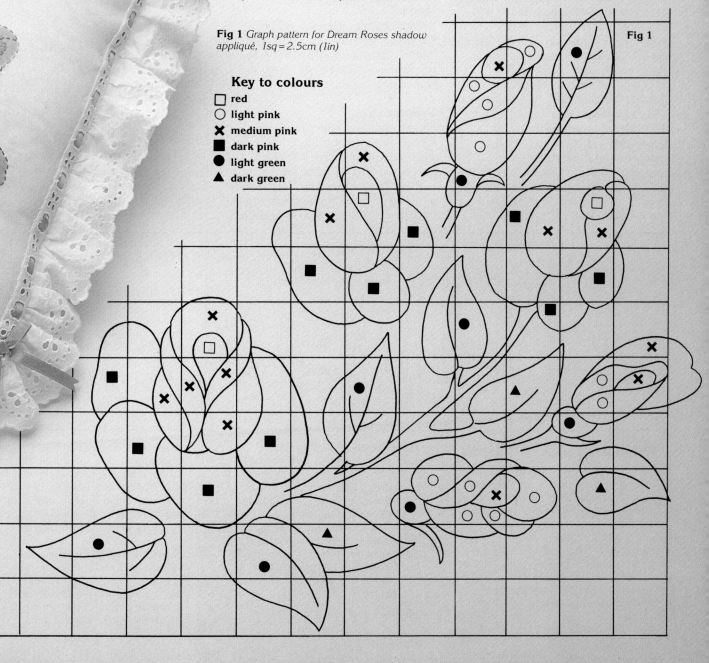

Fig 1

# Beading on lace

If you have never tried beading, working on lace is a good way to begin this fascinating and rewarding needlecraft. The pattern of the lace provides lines on which to work and the finished beadwork can have many uses — as decorative panels on fashion clothes, collars and cuffs, on belts and bags, or to make a beautiful keepsake, such as the wedding album cover in the picture.

## Tools and materials

**Lace** The heavier the lace, the easier it is to bead. Guipure motifs or all-over lace adapts best to the techniques of beading but fine laces can also be worked if the lace is mounted on fabric to provide sufficient weight and support.

**Threads** No. 50 sewing cotton thread is ideal for beading. Choose a colour to match the ground fabric and to harmonize with the beads. Pull cotton thread over a piece of beeswax or candle wax to smooth the thread and strengthen it for working. Invisible nylon thread can be used on fine nets and tulles.

**Needles** Beading needles are very fine and long and suited to the craft. Ordinary, slim sewing needles may be used but make sure that the threaded needle will pass easily through all the different types of beads.

## Choosing beads

The range of beads available is vast and it is all too easy to make the mistake of choosing several different types for a design. You will find it simpler to work a design if you limit your selection to about four types: three styles in the same colour range but in different shapes and one entirely different type of bead or sequin.

For instance, round pearl beads, flat pearly flowers and white crystal beads contrasting with silver sequins would make an effective range to work with.

## Preparation

All-over guipure lace can be put direct into an embroidery frame for working but take care not to tear the lace when fastening the frame.

Finer laces should be basted on to a background fabric before being put into an embroidery frame, and the

# Beading techniques

Six methods of attaching beads and sequins to fabric are shown. Start with a double backstitch on the wrong side of the work and finish in the same way. Do not draw threads up too tightly or the work will pucker. Beadwork should not be pressed but if it is absolutely necessary, press on the wrong side working on a pad or folded towel and avoid pressing over the beads or they may break.

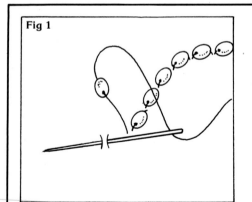

**Fig 1**

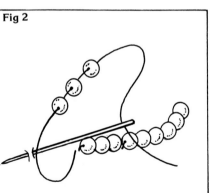

**Fig 2**

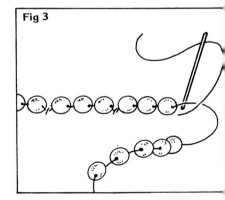

**Fig 3**

## Scatter effects (Fig 1)

Each bead is attached individually. Bring the needle through to the front of the work and pick up one bead. Slide it along the needle and just on to the thread, then pick up one thread of the background fabric the length of the bead along the design line. Draw the thread through to position the bead, then pick up the next bead on the needle.

## Straight lines (Fig 2)

Bring the needle through to the front of the work and pick up three or four beads. Slide them just on to the thread. Make a single running stitch, which positions the needle for the next group of beads to be picked up.

## Curved lines (Fig 3)

Two needles and thread are used at the same time. Thread beads on to needle and thread 1. Needle and thread 2 is used to make a couching stitch between groups of beads.

beading is worked through both layers.

Baste guipure motifs on a background fabric and then put the fabric into the frame.

The album cover in the picture has polyester wadding backing the fabric, which provided sufficient weight for the fabric to be worked without the use of an embroidery frame.

*Beadwork on the wedding album pictured (half the design is shown):*
**A** *Half pearl bead glued down*
**B** *Diamante stone glued down*
**C** *Flower-shaped pearl bead with crystal bead stitched through. The centre is a flat pearl bead with a crystal bead stitched through*
**D** *A half pearl bead is glued in the centre and surrounded with tiny pearl beads stitched through lace. Pearlised sequins are stitched to the centre of the petals*
**E** *Crystal beads are stitched to opalescent drops and to flower-shaped pearl beads. Tiny pearls and silver sequins make up the group*
**F** *A large pearl bead in the centre is surrounded by small pearl beads stitched through large octagonal crystal beads. Petals are filled with crystal beads and with small crystal beads stitched through flower-shaped pearl beads*
**G** *Crystal beads stitched through pearlised sequins*

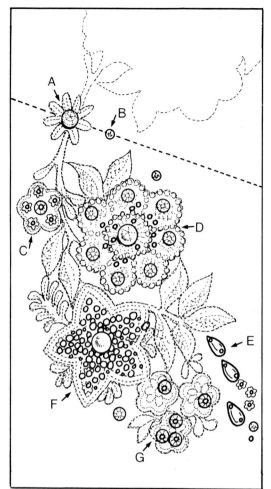

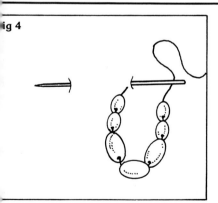

## Bead loops (Fig 4)

This technique can be used for decorative effects or as an edging.

Bring the needle through from the wrong side of the work and pick up sufficient beads to make the loop required. Pick up a thread of the fabric to secure the loop, ready for the next bead or beads.

Loops of beads can be fastened to the centre of a circle to make daisy effects, the petals lying free of the background fabric.

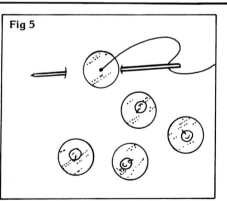

## Scatter sequins (Fig 5)

Single sequins can be attached in two ways. In method 1, bring the needle through from the wrong side, pass it through the sequin and then make a backstitch through the fabric. The sequin lies flat on the fabric and the needle is in position for the next sequin.

In method 2, bring the needle through from the wrong side, pass it through the sequin and then through a small bead. Pass the needle back through the hole in the sequin and

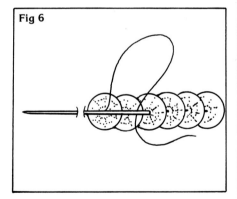

finish off the thread with a backstitch on the wrong side.

When attaching scatter sequins to lace or net, work several oversewing stitches round a single thread of the lace or net.

## Scale effects (Fig 6)

Bring the needle up through the hole in the sequin, set the sequin on the design line, then take a small stitch to the side of the sequin. Slip the next sequin on to the needle and do the same again.

# Embroidery on tulle

Tulle embroidery looks like lace and this delicate work can be used to make a wedding veil or perhaps an overdress for a baby gown. Mounted over a solid-colour fabric, tulle embroidery makes exquisite cushions.

The lovebirds and heart motif pictured could be repeated around the hem of a short or long veil, see page 99, or it could be used on the ends of an evening scarf.

Small pieces of embroidery are worked in an embroidery hoop but for large pieces, such as a veil, the tulle is mounted over soft cartridge or blotting paper and the work supported on a table top.

Pearl cotton, lace thread and stranded embroidery threads are all suitable for tulle embroidery. Needles should be blunt-tipped and pass easily through the holes in the tulle.

The basic stitches used in this embroidery are Running stitch, worked vertically, horizontally or diagonally, Stem stitch, Cording, and Darning stitch, with Buttonhole stitch used for edges. There are several filling stitches that are used for this work and some of them are based on ordinary embroidery stitches. Three are used in the lovebirds and heart motif: Wave stitch, Lattice Filling and Star Filling.

## Lovebirds and heart

### Materials required
*Finished motif size (without scalloped edge) 15 × 20cm (6 × 8in)*
40cm *(16in)* square silk or nylon tulle
White stranded embroidery thread
Tracing paper
Soft, dark blue paper (or other dark colour)
White watercolour paint and brush, or white pencil
Blunt-tipped needle
Embroidery hoop*

### Preparation
Trace the half-motif (Fig 1) on folded tracing paper, then re-trace the lines to obtain the whole motif as shown in the picture. Lay the tracing on the blue paper and draw over the lines

with a hard pencil, pressing firmly to mark the lines on the surface of the blue paper. Draw over the pressed marks with white paint or white pencil.

Baste the tulle over the design, making sure that a straight line of mesh holes runs down the centre of the heart. Place the mounted tulle in the embroidery hoop.
*If an embroidery hoop is not available, the mounted tulle can be basted to a piece of lightweight card, which will support the embroidery adequately.

### Working the design
To secure thread ends in tulle embroidery, the doubled thread is looped under a thread of the tulle and then the needle is passed back through the loop and the embroidery thread pulled tight (Fig 2). Long ends are left on the wrong side of the work and darned in after the embroidery is completed.

Outline the birds and the heart first in Running stitch using six

strands of thread in the needle. Do not work the wing and tail feathers at this stage.

The birds' breasts are worked in Darning stitch, using two strands of thread. Pass the needle in and out of mesh holes, going over, under, over, under tulle threads on the first row, then work a second row back in the same holes, going under threads where before you went over, and over where you went under. Follow the picture for shaping the Darning stitch area.

Work Wave stitch on the birds' wings and tails, using one strand of thread (Fig 3). Work Lattice Filling on the heart, using two strands of thread (Fig 4). Now work the wing and tail feathers in Running stitch, using six strands of thread. The birds' eyes and the flowers in the background are Star Fillings, using two strands of thread (Fig 5). The birds' beaks are worked with a few straight stitches, using one strand of thread.

The sprays of leaves under the birds are worked in Running stitch,

Fig 1

**Fig 1** *Half of the Lovebirds and Heart motif. Trace on folded tracing paper, then re-trace to obtain the complete design*

using two strands of thread. (Try to work an entire spray with one length, avoiding joins which would show.)

The 'ribbon' strands trailing from the heart and the ribbon loop and bow between the birds are also worked in Running stitch, using one strand of thread. The picots surrounding the heart are worked with a single strand of thread (see page 13 for method).

## Finishing

Outline the scallops with Running stitch, using six strands of thread. Then work Buttonhole stitch over the Running stitches, and another row of Running stitch just inside the scallops, both with three strands of thread.

Cut away the tulle close to the scallops. Unpick the basting stitches to remove the tulle embroidery from the pattern and darn in any thread ends on the back of the work.

**Fig 2**

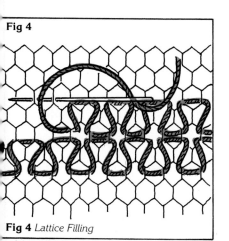

**Fig 2** *To secure thread ends, loop doubled thread under a mesh thread, pass the needle back through the loop and pull thread tight*

**Fig 3**

*(image showing Wave stitch)*

**Fig 3** *Wave stitch*

**Fig 4**

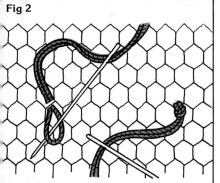

**Fig 4** *Lattice Filling*

**Fig 5**

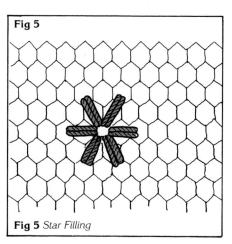

**Fig 5** *Star Filling*

## Making a wedding veil

For both short and long veils, tulle should be 1.85m (2yd) wide and you will need two separate lengths folded to make four layers.

For a short veil, measure from the crown of the head to the elbow and double the measurement. Buy two separate lengths to this measurement. Fold the two lengths in half across the width and work two rows of Running stitch along the fold, pulling them up to fit the veil on to the head-dress. A single layer of tulle is thrown forward over the face.

For a long veil, measure from the crown of the head to the floor and add the measurement from the crown to the elbow. You need two lengths of the total measurement. Round off the corners of both lengths. Fold them together across the width, at the crown to elbow measurement. Find the centre point on the fold. Mark a point 15cm (6in) each side of the centre and work Running stitch along this central 30cm (12in). Pull up the gathers to fit the head-dress.

The cut edges of tulle veils can be left unfinished, but a simple edging embroidery looks more professional.

# LACECRAFT TECHNIQUES 2

## Motifs from lace

Motifs cut from all-over lace can be used to embellish wedding clothes, evening wear, lingerie and decorative children's wear, and can look luxurious applied to hand-made bed linen.

1. Cut motifs from all-over lace, allowing 2.5cm (1in) all round.
2. Position the motifs on the background fabric, using stick adhesive on net or tulle fabrics and fine pins on other, woven fabrics.
3. Motifs can be applied to fabric by hand or by machine. Using hand-sewing, work tiny whip stitches on the edges of the motifs (see Lacecraft Techniques 1, page 88). To machine-stitch, set the work in an embroidery hoop and use a medium-size stitch just inside motif edges (see page 148).
4. When sewing is completed, trim away excess fabric around the motifs.

## Joining all-over lace

Pieces of all-over lace fabric or lengths of wide lace edging are joined with an appliqué technique. Either hand-sewing or machine-stitching can be used and, properly done, the finished join is virtually invisible.

1. Overlap the two pieces of lace, matching the pattern on the upper and lower layers, and pin together.
2. Working by hand, whip stitch (page 89) around the edges of the motif on the upper layer, stitching through to the motif on the lower layer (Fig 1).
3. Working by machine, first baste the two layers together, then stitch around the outline of the upper layer motif using a narrow zigzag stitch (page 148).
4. After stitching, trim away the excess fabric on both layers, close to the stitching.

**Fig 1**

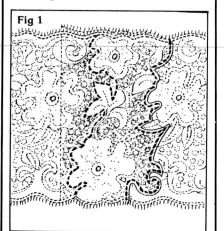

# Lace fascinator

Lace motifs are not always easily available but if an all-over lace fabric with a distinct pattern can be obtained, a short length will provide you with a number of motifs that can be cut out and used for appliqué.

The 'fascinator' shawl in the picture is made of cream spotted tulle appliquéd with motifs cut from Chantilly lace in a similar colour. The shaped border is made by 'invisibly' joining pieces of the same Chantilly lace. The technique of joining all-over lace is useful to learn and enables an expensive lace to be used more economically.

The technique for applying sequins to lace can be found on page 97. Alternatively, sequins can be applied with a touch of clear adhesive.

## Materials required

*Finished size 160cm (63in) on longest edge, 63cm (25in) at deepest point*
60cm (24in) of 120cm (48in)-wide cream tulle
60cm (24in) of 120cm (48in)-wide all-over cream Chantilly lace with large motifs
3m (3¼yd) of 10cm (4in)-wide cream lace edging
3m (3¼yd) of 1.5mm (¹⁄₁₆ in)-wide cream satin ribbon
7 lace butterfly motifs (optional)
1 packet of small pearlised sequins (optional)
Paste in solid stick form

## Preparation

Fold the tulle across the width. Measure and cut the fascinator (Fig 1). From the remaining tulle (shaded in Fig 1), cut three strips across the width 2.5cm (1in) wide.

From the Chantilly lace cut one strip across the width 15cm (6in) deep and then another strip to the same depth and about 66–71cm (26–28in) wide. These two pieces are to be joined at the ends, so it is important that the motifs on the ends match. Choose the area from which you will cut the second strip to achieve a matching motif.

From the remaining Chantilly lace cut out several motifs allowing approximately 2.5cm (1in) all round.

*At the turn of the century, lace fascinators were worn to cover the shoulders or as an evening head-covering*

**Fig 1** *Fold the tulle and cut out the fascinator on the fold*

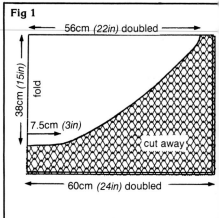

Fig 1

56cm (22in) doubled

38cm (15in)

fold

7.5cm (3in)

cut away

60cm (24in) doubled

## Working the design

Position the motifs on the tulle, working to within 2.5cm *(1in)* of the curved edge (see picture). Hold the motifs in position temporarily with a dab of adhesive. Stitch the motifs to the tulle (see Lacecraft Techniques 2, page 100).

Join the two strips of Chantilly lace (see Lacecraft Techniques 2, page 100), to make a strip 183cm *(72in)* long. With right sides together, pin and baste the Chantilly strip 6mm *(¼in)* inside the curved edge of the tulle, working from both ends towards the centre. Gather the middle 66cm *(26in)* and then finish pinning and basting the strip around the curved point of the fascinator.

Set the sewing machine to a narrow zigzag stitch and stitch the Chantilly lace to the tulle, first right sides together and then on the right side, working over the seam again.

Gather the lace edging (see Lacecraft Techniques 1, page 88). Baste the gathered lace along the bottom edge of the Chantilly lace strip, wrong side of lace edging to the right side of Chantilly lace, then topstitch using zigzag machine-stitching.

Join the three 2.5cm *(1in)*-wide strips of tulle on the short ends with zigzag stitch. Neaten both long edges of the strip with zigzag stitch. Machine-gather down the centre.

Baste the gathered strip over the join between the main fascinator piece and the Chantilly lace strip, and along the straight edge. Set the machine to a wide zigzag stitch. Stitch the gathered strip, working over the gathering line and catching in the narrow ribbon as you stitch. (Lay the ribbon on the seam line under the machine's presser foot and position the ribbon while stitching. If preferred, the ribbon can be couched down by hand (see page 70) after stitching down the gathered strip.)

## Finishing

Catch the lace butterfly motifs to the tulle, leaving the wing tips free of the fabric. Sew sequins at random over the lace motifs, on the gathered frill and along the hem (see picture). Alternatively, attach sequins with a touch of clear adhesive.

# Chapter Ten

# Appliqué

One of the chief charms of appliqué is its variety. There are several different techniques – including the use of ribbons, and combining appliqué with patchwork – and the kinds of designs you can create are limitless. You can use it for pictures and wallhangings or to decorate clothes for all the family, as well as practically everything in your home – bed-linen, cushions, table-linen.

'Appliqué' is the name given to the technique of placing pieces of fabric on to other fabrics and stitching them in place. This sounds like a very broad definition, but appliqué is an art with limitless expressions. It can be pictorial or abstract, bold and colourful or pale and delicate. Simple or complex designs can be created, depending on the number of different shapes you are laying on to the base fabric. You can also quilt the appliqué or add decorative embroidery to make your work extra-special. Appliqué has close links with both patchwork and quilting – techniques with which it is often combined.

Choosing the colours and textures of the fabrics and carefully planning an appliqué design is a skill in itself, and one which develops with practice.

## Using appliqué

The technique lends itself well to pictorial designs. Picture-painting with fabric is perhaps the most enjoyable and creative kind of appliqué. As it is so quick to do, areas can be covered comparatively fast, so appliqué is also suitable for furnishings – cushions, curtains, tablecloths, towels and blinds, even bed-covers. Colour co-ordinating in the home becomes easy and fun.

Sensational effects can be achieved on clothes. Adding the right motif can turn skirt hems, dresses, T-shirts, baby and children's wear into eye-catching designer originals.

## Types of appliqué

Appliqué can be hand or machine sewn. The choice will often depend on the desired finished effect or the function of the article you are making. The applied shapes can have either raw or turned edges. In this chapter you will discover several different types of appliqué and how and where to use them.

## Fabrics for appliqué

The fabrics used in appliqué are all-important. Choose them according to the project in hand. Obviously, if it is going to need washing, you must use washable, pre-shrunk, colour-fast fabrics. It would be very disappointing if parts of the design shrunk or lost their colour after one wash.

Fabrics should be of a similar weight if possible – particularly for anything which will receive hard wear or repeated

*Right: Successful appliqué needs well-chosen materials. Look out for suitable scraps of fabric, lace and trimmings.*

washing. For wallhangings and pictures this is not a problem, so you can go to town with pieces of silk and satin, velvets and other non-washables. Unless you want a translucent effect, make sure the fabric is densely woven. If it is too flimsy, it can be backed with a firmer fabric or with light iron-on interfacing to give it extra body and prevent the ground fabric from showing through. Firm cottons are always a good choice. Ribbon, braids and other trims can also be used to great effect in appliqué designs.

## Other equipment

**Scissors** You will need two pairs – one for cutting paper patterns, and a sharper pair for the fabric itself.

**Pins, needles and thread** are also indispensable.

**Stiff paper** is useful for making templates (patterns), as is tracing paper.

**Graph paper** is needed for enlarging and reducing designs.

**Tailor's chalk** or a pencil is used for marking shapes on to fabric. You could also use dressmaker's carbon paper for this.

**Frames** A frame is sometimes useful for working appliqué, but by no means essential. If you do use a frame, do not over-stretch the base fabric – keep all the fabrics at the same tension to avoid any puckering.

## Planning a simple appliqué

Shapes can be cut freely from the fabric, or else marked and cut accurately using paper patterns to enable you to repeat a design.

You can sometimes plan an appliqué design as you go along, but in general it's best to have a good idea of the effect you are after before starting work. Make sure that your chosen colours harmonize or contrast as you wish, and that none of the shapes is too complex. Remember that you can always add embroidery or machine stitching as part of the design. Books and pictures are a good source of designs for appliqué if you are not an artist. Try looking at young children's books for simple pictures with bold outlines.

# Kitchen pinboard with a country look

Make this useful pinboard to display small items such as postcards, notes, shopping lists and recipes. The colourful cow wandering across a meadow is made from remnants of fabric and mounted on thick polystyrene board. You can, of course, keep it as a picture if you don't want to stick pins in it.

## Materials required

*Finished size 60 × 70cm (24 × 28in)*
65cm (³⁄₄yd) cotton for background
35cm (³⁄₈yd) cotton for cow
40cm (¹⁄₂yd) cotton for border and
  hooves
(Note: fabric requirements are based on
  90cm (36in) width fabric)
Remnants for horns, udder and patches

Vilene Bondaweb
White and black embroidery silk
Sewing thread to match cotton fabric
  pieces
60 × 70cm (24 × 28in) polystyrene
  board 1cm (¹⁄₂in) thick
Double-sided adhesive tape

*Below: Co-ordinating fabrics are ideal.*

## Making the pinboard

Using the graph opposite, scale up the picture on to a sheet of paper. Trace individual shapes to make separate pattern pieces for each part of the cow. Cut a piece of background fabric 65 × 55cm (26 × 22in), plus 1cm (1/2in) seam allowance. Draw round the outline of the cow on the right side of background fabric, as a positioning guide.

Cut out the cow shape, patches, horns, hooves and tail from cotton fabric and place on Bondaweb. Iron to bond together. Remove backing, position cow on background fabric and iron in place. Add patches, horns, hooves and tail in the same way.

Zigzag stitch round the edges of all the pieces in the appropriate coloured cotton. This example uses white for the tail, mouth, ear and eye and blue for the horns. Work round any difficult shapes by hand, using buttonhole stitch. Embroider the cow's eye in embroidery silk. From plain fabric, cut two strips 10 × 70cm (4 × 28in) and two strips 10 × 80cm (4 × 32in). With right sides together sew the strips to the edges of the background fabric using a plain seam and mitring the corners (page 114). Press seams open.

Position the cow picture centrally on the polystyrene board using double-sided tape to secure it. Fold the excess material to the back of the board and stick down the edges with the tape.

## Chart for pinboard motif

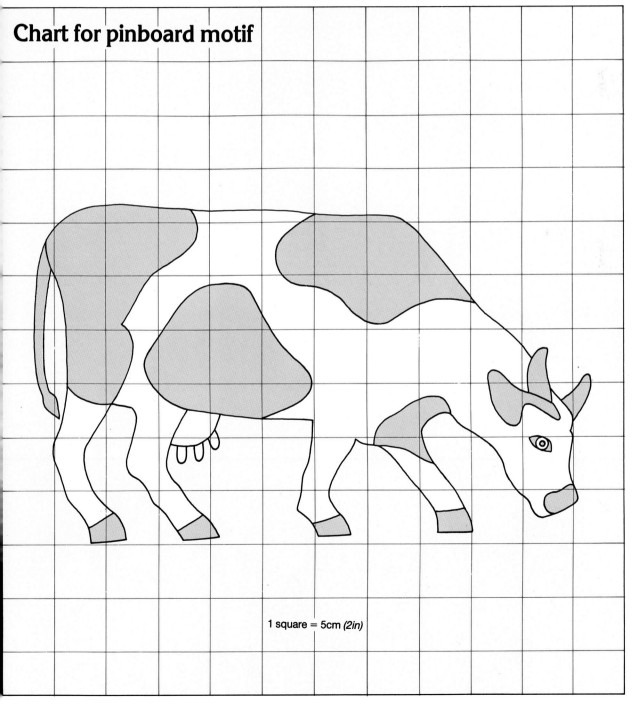

1 square = 5cm *(2in)*

# Baby's bib with ice-cream appliqué motif

This practical bib has a plastic backing for strength and practicality. The cheerful ice-cream motif adds a touch of colour to meal-times! For a wipe-clean bib, cover the front with transparent plastic sheeting.

## Materials required

*Finished size length 30cm (11¾in), width 25cm (9¾in)*
50cm *(20in)* of 90cm *(36in)* wide fabric
50cm *(20in)* of 90cm *(36in)* plastic backing fabric
1 packet bias binding
Fabric scraps for appliqué
Graph paper and tracing paper

## Making the bib

To make the pattern, draw a rectangle on a piece of graph paper to the size indicated on the diagram. Round off the corners to give an oval, as shown. Divide in half lengthwise, then mark in the points indicated and join them with

*Below: Baby can easily identify the bold and colourful motif.*

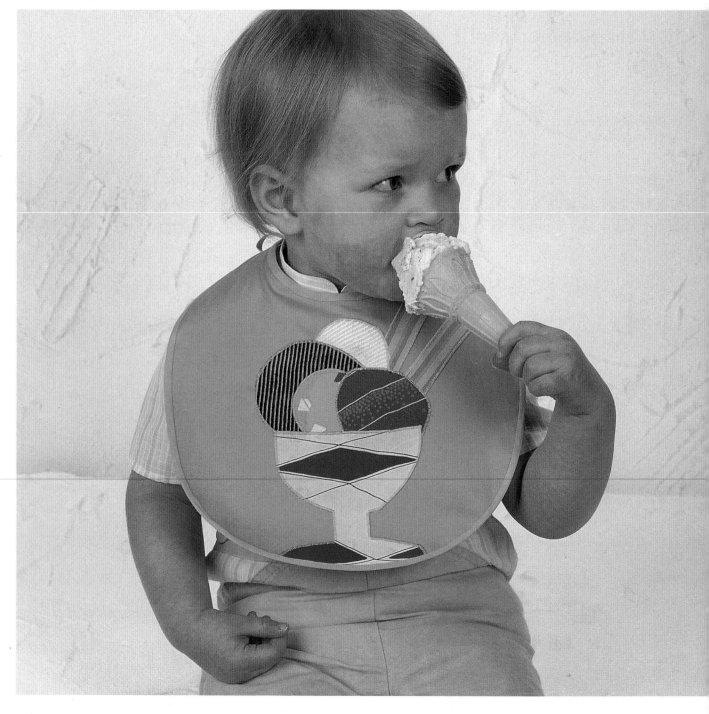

a smooth curve. Cut out the pattern along this curve, to scoop out the neckline. On a piece of tracing paper, trace off the ice-cream scoops, wafers and dish from the pattern given. Make individual pattern pieces for each piece.

To cut out, place pattern centre line on straight grain of fabric. Cut one bib piece from main fabric and one from plastic backing.

For the appliqué, choose fabric scraps in appropriate colours for ice-cream. Back each piece with iron-on interfacing, and cut out appliqué patches.

Place appliqué in position on the front of the bib, and tack to hold. Stitch to the bib, using machine satin stitch (page 148).

With wrong sides together, pin plastic backing to the bib. Cut a strip of bias binding to go around the outer edge. With right sides together, pin the binding to the front of the bib, and stitch, taking 5mm (¼in) turnings. Turn binding over to the back of the bib and slipstitch in place by catching along the row of machine stitching.

Cut another strip of bias binding, to measure the length of the neck edge plus 40cm (15½in). Leaving 20cm (7¾in) at either end for the ties, stitch binding to neck edge on front of bib. Turn binding under at neck edge and slipstitch to back of bib as before. Stitch together the folded edges of the extended binding, turning in the ends to neaten.

## Other appliqué ideas

This very simple form of appliqué leaves you with plenty of scope for bright bold designs. On the theme of food, think of the many easily recognisable snacks which could be adapted for an attractive motif. Choose something which is not too complicated, such as a hamburger or hot dog.

Draw the pattern carefully to a suitable size to fit the bib. To check that the design will work, colour it in using coloured pencils, particularly if you want to add extras, such as lettuce or ketchup. Or you could give the bib a pop art look by applying replicas of tins or other food packaging: obvious ones to choose are baked bean or soup tins or yogurt cartons. You may need to use fabric markers for the writing, or embroider the words.

# Trace pattern for ice-cream motif

## Trace pattern for ice-cream motif

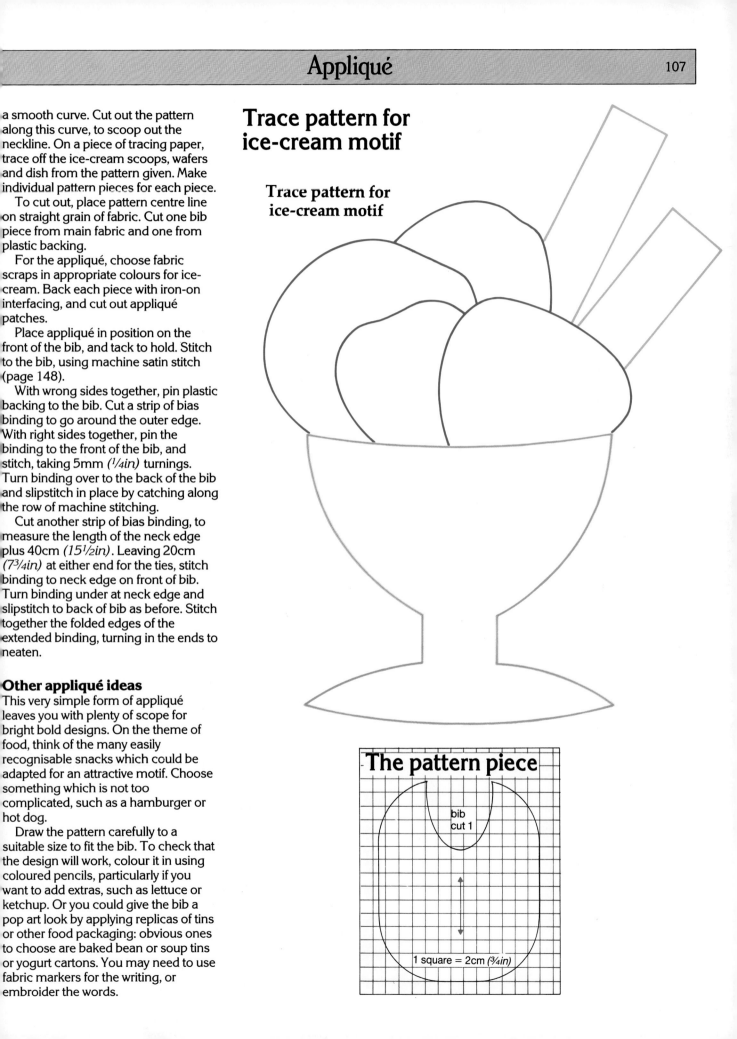

## The pattern piece

bib
cut 1

1 square = 2cm (¾in)

# RIBBON APPLIQUÉ

Appliqué is the term used for applying a small piece of fabric to a larger piece, but when the term is used for ribbon a whole range of new ideas and techniques becomes possible. Once you begin to think of ribbon as a narrow fabric with two edges already finished off for you, ribbon becomes the simplest material to use for decoratively banding garments and house furnishings.

Developing the idea, ribbon need not be stitched down on both edges − it can be left partially free of the background fabric. The finished edges also mean that embroidery stitches can be used to apply ribbons − by hand or by machine − and this leads to ideas about couching ribbons. At this point, the enthusiastic needlewoman has evolved ideas for gathering, pleating, twisting, knotting, plaiting and shirring ribbon and applying it to background fabric in dozens of ways. The ribbon appliqué samplers on pages 110–11 show just a few ways in which ribbon can be used for applied decorative effects.

## Types of ribbons

Only polyester ribbons should be used for appliqué if the finished item is to be washed or dry-cleaned.

Ribbons are available in a vast range of colours, textures and patternings. Satins and grosgrains can be plain or woven into stripes and Jacquards. Ribbons come printed with spots or with decorative motifs such as flowers, hearts, stars, ships, whales and anchors − or with familiar characters such as Snoopy and Woodstock. Jacquard ribbons can be prettily floral or brilliant and striking with touches of glitter. Lurex ribbons in silver, gold, pewter and copper provide opportunities for dramatic effects, while polyester velvet ribbons add a luxurious dimension to appliqué designs.

## Working with ribbons

Although reputable brands of polyester ribbons are washable, it is always advisable to launder both ribbons and the background fabric before using them for appliqué.

Ribbons should be basted rather than pinned in position, working basting along both selvedges because once pinholes are made in ribbon it is virtually impossible to remove them.

Ribbons can be stitched down by hand or by machine, using straight, zigzag or embroidery stitches (see page 110). Using straight machine stitches, always work in the same direction on both edges to minimise puckering. A commercial bonding material is available which makes ribbon appliqué very easy. It is made in four ribbon widths and is simply laid along placement lines, the ribbon positioned on top and then ironed on to the fabric. The ribbon adheres smoothly and machine-stitching can then be worked without basting. Polyester ribbons should not require pressing after appliqué but if it is necessary, make sure that all the basting threads (and pins) are removed first.

*Ribbons, lace and broderie (eyelet) used together give a rich but fresh feeling in bedroom furnishings. The tucked bedcover is made from white sheeting, with a deep broderie (eyelet) frill trimmed with ribbon-threaded lace and piped with polyester satin ribbon. Matching pillows have wide frills appliquéd with narrow ribbon.*

Photograph: Pins and Needles Magazine

# Appliqué samplers

Here are just a few of the dozens of ways in which ribbon can be applied to fabric to produce colourful or pretty effects. Try each of them as a sampler for your own library of appliqué ideas – and others are sure to occur to you.

Embroidery stitches can be used to appliqué ribbons to fabrics adding an extra dimension to your work. For instance, you could use a different coloured or textured thread, or simply by working a decorative stitch the effect will change – Herringbone, Chain and Satin (variations) and Buttonhole can all be used. Bear in mind the size of your project when choosing how to appliqué your ribbons – you may not want to spend hours hand-appliquéing vast lengths of ribbons, while on the other hand a small project would be greatly enhanced by hand embroidery.

*Top left:* 23mm (⅞in)-wide satin ribbon is pleated and stitched to the ground fabric. 7mm (¼in)-wide ribbon is overlaid down the middle and stitched on both edges to hold pleats to fabric. The appliqué band is then pressed.
*Centre:* 23mm (⅞in)-wide satin ribbon is gathered on one edge and stitched to the ground fabric. 7mm (¼in)-wide ribbon is laid along the gathers and stitched on both edges.
*Bottom right:* pleated 23mm (⅞in)-wide satin ribbon is stitched to fabric through a flat plait of 1.5mm (¹⁄₁₆in)-wide ribbon (Fig 1).

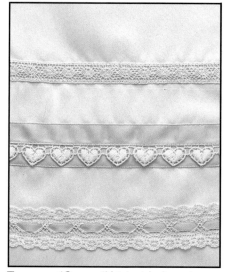

*Top row:* 13mm (½in)-wide lace is overlaid on satin ribbon of the same width and stitched along both edges of the lace through the ribbon to the ground fabric.
*Centre row:* 13mm (½in)-wide satin ribbon is stitched on both edges and guipure lace is laid over it. A second piece of ribbon is placed above the first and over the straight edge of the lace. It is then stitched down.
*Bottom row:* eyelet or beading lace is threaded with ribbon and stitched to the ground fabric.

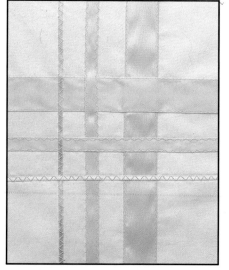

Satin ribbons of different widths are laid and interwoven, each ribbon being stitched as it is applied. Wide ribbons are stitched with straight stitches, medium-width ribbons with zigzag machine-stitch. Very narrow ribbons are couched down with zigzag stitches.

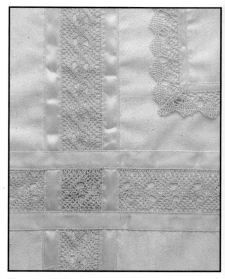

Textured interest is achieved with thick cotton lace and satin ribbons. 3cm (1¼in)-wide lace is set in a cross. 13mm (½in)-wide ribbon is laid over lace vertically and stitched on both edges, then horizontally and stitched.
*Above right:* 7mm (¼in)-wide ribbon is appliquéd along straight edge of lace trim.

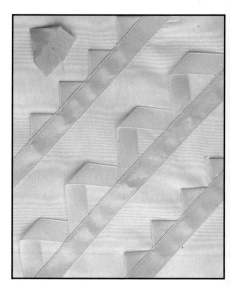

*Top left and bottom right:* triangles of satin ribbon are folded and pressed (as turquoise sample), then basted to the ground fabric. A strip of ribbon is laid on the edge of the triangles and stitched on both edges to the ground fabric.
*Centre:* regular zigzag folds in satin ribbon are pressed, then basted to the ground fabric. A strip of ribbon of the same width is stitched over the bottom edge of the zigzag strip.

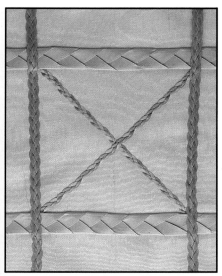

Three pieces of 10mm (³⁄₈in)-wide pink satin ribbon are fold-plaited (Fig 2) and hand-sewn to the ground fabric. The lilac and multi-coloured satin ribbons are flat-plaited (Fig 1) and hand-sewn to the ground fabric.

*Top row:* a bow of flat-plaited 3mm (¹⁄₈in)-wide grosgrain ribbon is stitched to a hand-applied band of flat plait (Fig 1).
*Centre row:* a stitched satin ribbon bow is hand-sewn to a machine-applied ribbon of the same width.
*Bottom row:* a simple loop bow of 7mm (¹⁄₄in)-wide grosgrain ribbon is hand-sewn to an applied strip of the same width.

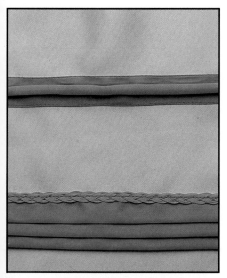

*Top row:* 23mm (⁷⁄₈in)-wide satin ribbon is folded lengthwise. The fold is machine-stitched and pressed. The ribbon is then machine-stitched on both edges to the ground fabric and pressed flat.
*Bottom row:* three pieces of 23mm (⁷⁄₈in)-wide satin ribbon are folded lengthwise and the fold pressed. The three pieces are laid with folds overlapping and each machine-stitched on the top edge to the ground fabric. A flat plait (Fig 1) trims the top row.

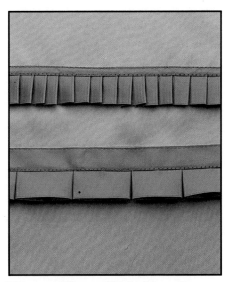

*Top row:* 23mm (⁷⁄₈in)-wide satin ribbon is knife-pleated, basted to the ground fabric and pressed. 7mm (¹⁄₄in)-wide ribbon is stitched along the top edge.
*Bottom row:* box pleats are pressed into 23mm (⁷⁄₈in)-wide satin ribbon and basted to the ground fabric. 16mm (⁵⁄₈in)-wide ribbon is stitched along the top edge.

# Ribbon plaits or braids

Plaited or braided ribbon is a very pretty form of ribbon appliqué. It can be machine- or hand-stitched, depending on the effect required, and can be worked in single or massed rows.

As a ribbon plait is flexible, it can be used where ordinary ribbon appliqué would be impossible, such as on the hem of a circular skirt or round a collar. Ribbon plaits make very good ties for belts and strong, yet pretty, straps for bags and purses. They also make non-slip straps for lingerie.

Two different plaits are possible with ribbons, the flat plait and the folded plait. The flat plait can be worked only with 1.5mm and 3mm (¹⁄₁₆in and ¹⁄₈in)-wide ribbon. The folded technique can be worked on ribbon up to 13mm (¹⁄₂in) wide.

Fig 1 shows how the flat plait is worked. The ribbons are brought forward without folding. Fig 2 shows the folded plait where ribbons are folded forward at each stage of the plaiting. Allow one-third more ribbon than the required finished length of the plait and pin all three ribbons together to a board or table top to plait.

Ribbon plaits should be pressed when they are completed.

Fig 1

Fig 2

# Scatter cushions

Each of the cushions is designed to make effective use of ribbons of different widths. Many ribbon colours – subtle pale tints, fresh, bright colours and rich, dark shades – can be obtained as wide as 77mm *(3in)* through a range of sizes to a narrow 1.5mm *(1/16 in)*. This enables the creative needlewoman to work with wide ribbons as though they were

## Making cushion covers the easy way

Making cushion covers is simple if you use a 'pillow opening' instead of a zip fastener. The technique can be used on cushions and pillows of any shape and can also be adapted to duvet covers.

Cut the back of the cushion cover to the same depth as the front but 10cm *(4in)* wider. Cut the piece in two from top to bottom. Press a narrow fold to the wrong side on these cut edges. Fold again to make a 2.5cm *(1in)* hem. Stitch. Lay the two pieces together, overlapping the hemmed edges so that the cushion back is now the same width as the cushion front. Baste them together all round, right sides facing, then stitch. Turn 'o right side through the opening. The opening can be fastened with a button and thread loop, snap fasteners or ribbon ties.

### Frilled edges

Applying a frilled or lace edge is easier when following the pillow opening method for a cushion cover. Gather the straight edge of the frill and fit it round the front cushion piece, allowing a little extra fullness at the corners. Join the short ends.

Pin and baste the gathered frill to the right side of the cushion front, arranging it so that the join is at a corner. The straight edge of the frill should lie along the edge of the cushion.

Lay the prepared cushion back on top, right side down. Baste all round, then stitch. Turn the cushion cover to the right side through the back opening.

*Designed by Alison Palmer*

pieces of fabric and then trim her work with the same colours in narrow ribbons. The Blue Balloons and the Cream and Mint cushions show the scope of ribbon appliqué.

# Blue balloons

## Materials required
*Finished size 30cm (12in) square*
2 pieces of 33cm *(13in)* square white polyester satin fabric
1.60m *(1¾yd)* of 10cm *(4in)*-wide white broderie anglaise (eyelet) edging
Copen Blue 335 single face polyester satin ribbons as follows: 20cm *(8in)* of 77mm *(3in)*-wide; 80cm *(31in)* of 16mm *(⅝in)*-wide; 1.40m *(1½yd)* of 7mm *(¼in)*-wide
30cm *(12in)* square cushion pad
Scraps of polyester wadding
Matching Drima sewing threads

## Preparation
On thin card draw a rectangle 68mm *(2⅝in)* deep by 55mm *(2⅛in)* wide. Round off between the lines to make an oval shape to these dimensions. Cut out the oval for a template for the balloon shapes. Trace three balloons on to the wide Copen Blue 335 ribbon, about 1cm *(⅜in)* apart. Machine-stitch round the outlines with a narrow zigzag stitch. Cut out the three shapes with about 3mm *(⅛in)* allowance all round.

Position the balloons (as shown in the picture) on a square of white satin fabric. Baste in position, using a fine needle and keeping the stitches near the edge. (A coarse needle or pins will make holes that are impossible to remove.)

## Working the appliqué
Work close zigzag stitch round the balloons, leaving a small gap at the bottom of each balloon. Push a little wadding into the balloons, using a knitting needle. Cut three 17cm *(7in)* lengths of 7mm *(¼in)*-wide ribbon. Tuck one end into each balloon and oversew. Make three small ribbon bows from the same ribbon and sew one under each balloon.

## Applying trim
**Making square corners** Cut the broderie (eyelet) into four equal pieces. Lay two pieces together, right

sides facing (Fig 1). Fold one end at an angle of 45 degrees. Press. Stitch on the fold line. Trim off the corner. Open the broderie (eyelet) and press the seam open. Trim to make a neat square corner. Join all four pieces in the same way. Stitch the broderie (eyelet) 'frame' to the cushion piece.

**Making mitred corners** Apply 16mm (⅝in)-wide ribbon over the straight edges of the broderie (eyelet) square, mitring the corners neatly (Fig 2). Pin the ribbon in position, then edge-stitch along the inner edge. When you get to the corner, fold the ribbon back on itself and then diagonally to the side, making a right angle. Press the fold and then stitch on the crease through the ribbon and the fabric underneath. Open out the ribbon and press flat. Continue edge-stitching along the same inner edge until you reach the next corner. Work all four corners in the same way, then finish by sewing the outer edge of the ribbon all round.

## Finishing

Bring the three ribbons from the balloons to one corner. Stitch down. Trim the ends so that the ribbons are of similar length, then cut each into a fish tail.

Make a bow from the remaining ribbon and sew over ribbons.

Make up the cushion as described in the box on page 112.

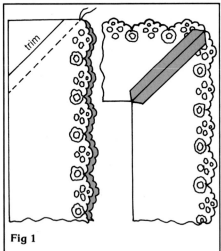

**Fig 1** *Square corner*

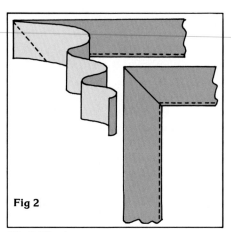

**Fig 2** *Mitred corner*

## Lilac heart

### Materials required

*Finished size 30×35cm (12×14in)*

2 pieces of 40cm (16in) square white polyester satin fabric

1m (1⅛yd) of 10cm (4in)-wide white broderie anglaise (eyelet) edging

3m (3¼yd) of 7cm (2¾in)-wide white broderie anglaise (eyelet) edging

Light Orchid 430 single face polyester satin ribbons as follows: 1m (1⅛yd) of 23mm (⅞in)-wide and 13mm (½in)-wide; 35cm (14in) of 7mm (¼in)-wide

80cm (31in) of 23mm (⅞in)-wide Light Orchid 430 double face polyester satin ribbon

30×35cm (12×14in) heart-shaped cushion pad

Matching Drima sewing threads

### Preparation

Use the cushion pad to draw a heart-shaped paper pattern. Cut out two shapes from white satin, adding 2cm (¾in) seam allowance all round. On one piece mark a vertical centre line in chalk.

### Working the design

Cut two 28cm (11in) lengths of wide broderie (eyelet) edging. Lay the pieces together, fold one end diagonally and stitch to make a square corner (Fig 1). Sew to cushion piece with the decorative edge towards the bottom of the heart and aligning the join with the chalked centre line. Cut the remaining wide broderie (eyelet) into two equal lengths and stitch to make a square corner. Cut the narrowest Light Orchid 430 ribbon into two equal lengths and thread through the eyelet holes of both pieces of the broderie (eyelet), fastening ribbon ends off on the wrong side with two or three stitches. Position and stitch on the cushion so that the decorative edge is towards the top of the heart.

Cut both the 23mm and 13mm (⅞in and ½in)-wide ribbons in two pieces and cut and seam to make square corners. Appliqué the ribbons over the straight edges of the broderie (eyelet).

## Finishing
Pleat the narrower broderie (eyelet) and baste to fit around the cushion. Apply the frill and make up the cushion as described in the box on page 112.

Make a bow from the double face Light Orchid 430 ribbon and hand-sew at top of heart.

# Rose pink and cream cushion

## Materials required
*Finished size 24×30cm (9½×12in)*
2 pieces of 28×33cm (11×13in)
  cream polyester satin fabric
4m (4½yd) of 4cm (1½in)-wide
  cream broderie anglaise (eyelet)
  edging
Pink 150 single face polyester satin
  ribbons as follows: 35cm (14in) of

39mm (1½in)-wide; 70cm (28in) of 23mm (⅞in)-wide and 16mm (⅝in)-wide
24×30cm (9½×12in) cushion pad
Matching Drima sewing threads

## Preparation
Mark the centre line lengthwise along one piece of satin fabric. Cut six 35cm (14in) lengths of broderie (eyelet) edging.

## Working the design
Baste a strip of broderie (eyelet) on both long sides of the cushion piece 2cm (¾in) from the edge. Lay a piece of the narrowest Pink 150 ribbon over both the straight edges and stitch along both edges of ribbon. Now lay a strip of broderie (eyelet) so that the decorative edge just overlaps the ribbons and baste.

Cut the 23mm (⅞in)-wide ribbon in two equal pieces and stitch over the straight edge of the broderie (eyelet) strips. Baste the last two strips of broderie (eyelet) so that they just overlap the ribbon. Appliqué the widest piece of ribbon down the centre, to cover the raw edges of the last two strips of broderie (eyelet).

## Finishing
Cut the remaining broderie (eyelet) into four equal pieces. Make a square by following the technique described for Blue Balloons cushion (see also Fig 1). Pleat and baste the frill to fit around the cushion.

Apply the frill and make up the cushion as described in the box on page 112

# Cream and mint cushion

## Materials required
*Finished size 28.5cm (11¼in) square*
2 pieces of 33cm (13in) square cream
  polyester satin fabric
1m (1⅛yd) of 57mm (2¼in)-wide
  and 60cm (24in) of 10mm (⅜in)-
  wide Mint 530 single face
  polyester satin ribbon
1m (1⅛yd) of 57mm (2¼in)-wide
  and 30cm (12in) of 10mm (⅜in)-
  wide Cream 815 single face
  polyester satin ribbon
1.20m (1⅜yd) of 5cm (2in)-wide
  cream broderie anglaise (eyelet)
  edging

Square cushion pad
Matching Drima sewing threads

## Preparation
On one piece of satin fabric mark a line diagonally from corner to corner and then across again in the opposite direction, from corner to corner. Draw a plan on paper to size, following Fig 3. Cut out triangle A and segment B and use these as patterns for cutting ribbons.

## Working the design
Work the four centre triangles first. From the wide ribbon cut two in Cream 815 and two in Mint 530, adding 6mm (¼in) turnings on the raw edges.

Position a Cream 815 triangle on the satin fabric, then turn raw edges under. Baste and stitch the bottom edge only. Prepare and position the second Cream 815 triangle to the right of the first, just overlapping the edge, and stitch the bottom edge and the left side. Now prepare and work the first Mint 530 triangle, again to the right, and stitch bottom edge and left side. Work the last Mint 530 triangle, machining all three sides.

Appliqué the 10mm (⅜in)-wide ribbon round the square, as shown in Fig 3, folding to make mitred corners (Fig 2). Cut and work the four segments B in the same way and in the same order as the triangles. Stitch top and bottom edges of piece 1, then top, bottom and left edge of piece 2, and so on.

## Finishing
Make small bows with the remaining narrow Mint 530 ribbon and stitch on opposite corners, as shown in the picture.

Cut the broderie (eyelet) into four equal pieces. Make a square by following the technique described for Blue Balloons cushion (see also Fig 1). Stitch to cushion front, matching straight edge of trim to outer edge of ribbon appliqué.

Make up the cushion as described in the box on page 112.

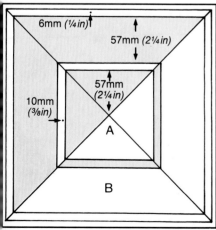

**Fig 3** *Appliqué plan for Cream and Mint Cushion, showing triangles and segments*

# Lace and ribbon quilt

Lace and ribbons are lovely materials to work with in appliqué. As you are working with two selvedges, stitching is easy and the work grows quickly. The panel of appliqué in the picture is for a quilt made up of 23cm (9in) squares of lace and ribbons. The centre square shown is appliquéd with antique cotton lace set around a square of ribbon weaving.

The quilt is made up of 45 whole squares and 22 half squares (see Fig 1). You could vary all the appliqué squares, mixing and matching together laces and ribbons of different widths and colour tones.

## Materials required

*Finished size 255×152cm (100×60in)*

2.60m (2⅞yd) of 157cm (62in)-wide cream polyester cotton or satin for backing

4.60m (5yd) of 114cm (45in)-wide thin cream cotton fabric for mounting appliqué

2.60m (2⅞yd) of 157cm (62in)-wide polyester wadding (optional)

Assorted laces and ribbons of different widths in cream, tan and ivory colour ranges*

14m (15⅜yd) of 16mm (⅝in)-wide Cream 815 single face polyester satin ribbon for joining squares

Lace trim (optional – see Edging the quilt)

Matching Drima sewing threads

**\*Each square of appliqué takes nine pieces of 2.5cm (1in)-wide lace or ribbon, so allow a total of 2.30m (2½yd) per square**

## Preparation

Cut the thin cotton into 56 squares. Cut 11 of the squares in half on the diagonal. Work each square or half square separately. Cut ribbons and lace into 23cm (9in) lengths.

## Working the design

Pin and baste ribbons and lace to the squares, edges touching. You can mix lace and ribbons of different widths and colours. If you have odd scraps of lace net, try basting a piece over the backing square without ribbons or lace strips for a textural contrast. Work all the squares and half squares. Trim the backing fabric to the edges of the appliqué.

## Joining squares

Lay two squares together, right sides facing. Join along one edge with large oversewing stitches, worked right on the edge, as a basting. Join enough squares to make a strip, then press on the right side. Stitch over the basted seam with zigzag stitches.

Join all the squares together, with the half squares on the edges of the quilt. Stitch the 16mm (⅝in)-wide Cream 815 ribbon over the joins with straight stitches along both edges of the ribbons.

## Finishing

Lay the backing fabric wrong side up. If you are using polyester wadding, place this on the backing. Lay the appliqué on top, right side up. Pin the corners, then the edges. Thread the needle with a doubled length of thread. Tie a knot on the end. Make two or three stitches right through the appliqué top to the backing, at the corners of all the squares. Trim the knot and finish on the wrong side with a back stitch to secure. These are called 'quilting ties'.

If you prefer a decorative tie, use 1.5mm (1/16 in)-wide Cream 815 ribbon. Work from the right side and bring the needle back to the right side, tying the ends in a tight bow.

## Edging the quilt

The quilt may be edged in a variety of ways. A double frill of cream lace would look very glamorous. You would need about 16.50m (18yd) to make a double layer of pre-frilled lace edging. Alternatively, a single frill of cream broderie anglaise (eyelet) might be used; for this you would need 8.25m (9yd). A simple lace insert with a ribbon to match the quilt could be applied to the edge; again, allow 8.25m (9yd) of each. Or perhaps a single wide band of Cream 815 satin ribbon with mitred corners might be used; you would need 8.25m (9yd) of 39mm (1½in)-wide ribbon.

Having applied the trim of your choice, turn the edges of the backing fabric under and hand-hem to the back of the quilt.

Designed by Audrey Vincente Dean

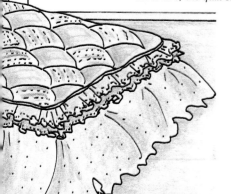

Fig 1 *Diagram of the Lace and Ribbon Quilt, made up of 45 whole squares and 22 half squares. The dark shaded area is the centre square; the light shaded rectangle represents the area of the quilt shown in the picture*

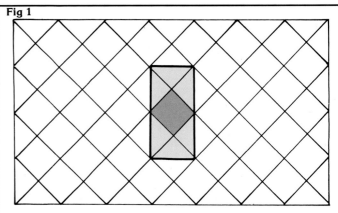

**Fig 1**

# PATCHWORK AND APPLIQUÉ

Patchwork and appliqué go hand in hand in quilt-making, the straight lines of seamed patchwork contrasting with the freedom of cut-out fabric shapes sewn to a foundation fabric. Crazy patchwork, the oldest of the techniques used to make new fabric from old, is still a thrifty craft and can be worked with different kinds of fabric to make items that are both beautiful and useful. You will find more about patchwork in Chapter Eleven.

## Crazy patchwork

The technique of sewing together small scraps of good fabric to make a larger piece has been practised for hundreds of years. Early examples of crazy patchwork were made of pieces of woollen fabric sewn together over a foundation fabric to make warm bed covers. Crazy patchwork as a decorative form of needlework, used to make dramatic quilts like the one pictured, evolved in the mid-nineteenth century.

The quilt pictured was made in the United States of America in the 1880s and is unusual in that it has been constructed from 12 blocks of patchwork, each individually worked and measuring 30cm (12in) square.

### Fabrics

Although almost any kind of fabric can be used for crazy patchwork it is advisable to choose pieces of uniform thickness. If crazy patchwork is intended for making fashion garments or accessories that are likely to be subjected to heavy wear, it may be better to buy new fabrics, as partially-worn cloth may pull away from the stitches.

Foundation fabrics should be new; closely woven cotton is recommended.

The backing fabric, on which the crazy patchwork is mounted, can be of almost any type – velvet, woven wool, needlecord, brocade, heavy satin, twilled fabric or cotton – provided that it is of sufficient weight to support the patchwork.

### Threads

All-purpose polyester thread is recommended for sewing the patches on to the foundation fabric. Stranded cotton or lustrous embroidery cotton are both suitable for the surface decoration. Tapisserie wools can also be used for textural contrast.

### Preparation

Clean and press all patchwork fabrics. Iron creases from the foundation fabric.

### Working the design

Although crazy patchwork may look haphazard in design, consideration must be given to the position of patches to achieve a pleasing balance of colour, texture and pattern.

Cut pieces of the patchwork fabrics to the size required and lay them on the foundation fabric, moving them around until a harmonious effect is achieved. Starting at a corner, trim the first selected piece to a right angle. Pin it to the corner, then work running stitches around the right angle, taking stitches through the foundation fabric (Fig 1).

Slip the next patch about 12mm (½in) under the edge of the first. Work running stitches around the edges of both patches, leaving the front edges free so that you can slip more patches underneath (Fig 2). Continue adding patches, slipping them under the edges of previous patches and sewing securely to the foundation fabric through all layers. Work across the foundation fabric until it is covered.

### Embroidery

Any kind of stitch can be used in crazy patchwork. Stitches are worked over the raw edges of all the patches to secure them and to make a decorative effect. The quilt pictured uses Chain Stitch, Feather Stitch, Herringbone Stitch, Buttonhole Stitch and Cretan Stitch.

### Finishing

Mount the finished patchwork on a backing fabric (see page 136 for the technique).

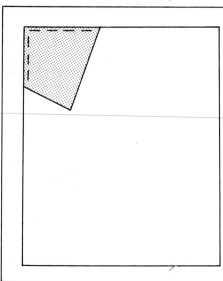

**Fig 1** *Trim the first patch to a right angle and sew to a corner*

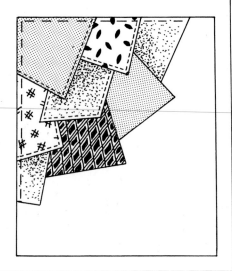

**Fig 2** *Slip patches under the edges of the first, then sew through all layers, leaving the front edges free for inserting more patches*

# Friendship quilt

Making Friendship Quilts is an American tradition and one of the most charming of communal sewing projects.

In the days of the early American pioneers, young girls, who were engaged to be married, set to stitching quilts and covers for their future homes. Twelve quilts were considered sufficient to set up housekeeping but a thirteenth quilt was made by the betrothed girl's friends, each working a block of appliqué or patchwork. The blocks were designed in a variety of ways, illustrating events from the girl's life, or depicting flowers, insects and animals from the locality.

At the final quilting bee, an important social occasion in the community and to which the men were sometimes invited, the blocks were 'set', joined with strips of fabric or prepared patchwork, and then the quilt was mounted in a frame for hand-quilting.

The modern quilt in the picture was made for an American girl living in England by friends in a local quilting group. It was designed by the owner in three main colours: green, white and pink. A free hand was given to those making the blocks, working within this colour scheme. Some of the blocks are made in traditional patterns, others have been adapted and are loosely based on popular designs (Fig 1).

The quilt measures 218×142cm (86×56in) and each of the rectangular blocks is 22×29cm (8½×11½in). The blocks are set in strips of green and white fabric. The outer strips surrounding the blocks are made up of 5cm (2in) green squares at the corners, white rectangles measuring 29×5cm (11½×2in) and green rectangles measuring 10×5cm (4×2in). The inner strips are wider: the green squares are 10cm (4in) and the green and white rectangles are 29×10cm (11½×4in). The completed patchwork quilt is bordered with a 10cm (4in) band in green fabric.

Quilting has been worked on the blocks and linking strips to add texture. The traditional Twisted Ropes design is used for some of the quilting (Fig 2).

**Fig 1**

| | | |
|---|---|---|
| 1 | 2 | 3 |
| 4 | 5 | 6 |
| 7 | 8 | 9 |
| 10 | 11 | 12 |
| 13 | 14 | 15 |
| 16 | 17 | 18 |

**Fig 1** *Key to the designs of the blocks that make up the Friendship Quilt pictured:*
*1 Elongated Star* **2** *Twin Sisters* **3** *Dutchman's Puzzle* **4** *Rail Fence* **5** *Dresden Plate* **6** *Adaptation of Windmill* **7** *Birds and Flowers* **8** *Woven Ribbons* **9** *Double Hearts* **10** *Checkerboard* **11** *Adaptation of Fan* **12** *Star* **13** *House* **14** *Squared pattern* **15** *Tulips* **16** *Log Cabin* **17** *Flower* **18** *Log Cabin*

**Fig 2** *Twisted Ropes quilting design*

**Fig 2**

# Patchwork motifs

Pieces of patchwork can be used as appliqué motifs to decorate clothes and accessories, and home furnishings. Hexagons, sewn into rosettes, or the Ocean Wave pattern on page 132, make pretty borders. Diamonds, triangles and squares are all suitable for grouping into motifs.

## Preparation

After sewing patches together, press on the wrong side with the papers still in position. If the right side of work needs pressing, unpick the basting stitches but leave the papers in place. Dry-press over a thin cloth. If the patchwork fabrics are thin and the turnings show through on the right side, it will be necessary to line the entire piece or to cut 'papers' from cotton lining fabric or thin, non-woven interfacing and insert them under the turnings before working appliqué.

## Lining motifs

Pin the pressed patchwork to a piece of cotton lining fabric and pencil round the shape. Cut out the lining 6mm *(¼in)* away from the pencilled line. Press open the turnings on the edges of the patchwork. Baste the patchwork to the lining, right side down. Machine-stitch on the pencilled line, leaving a small gap for turning to the right side. Close the open seam with slipstitches and press the lined motif ready for appliqué.

## Mounting appliqué

Appliqué can be worked either by hand or by machine. To hand-sew, work tiny slipstitches through the edge of the patchwork motif (Fig 1). Machine-stitching can either be done with a small straight stitch, worked right on the edge of the patchwork, or with an open zigzag stitch (page 148).

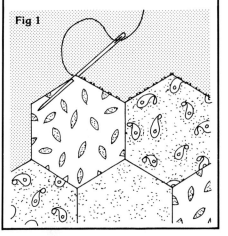

**Fig 1**

# Country cottage

The picture combines two techniques, traditional English patchwork using hexagons and appliqué for the cottage and path. The hexagons are worked as a mosaic of plain and patterned fabrics chosen to represent trees, flowers and foliage, sky and clouds. In places, diamonds and smaller hexagons have been superimposed on hexagons to add detail or more interest to the pattern.

## Working the design

The panel measures 91×60cm *(36×24in)* and is made up of approximately 225 hexagons worked with a 2.5cm *(1in)* template.

The trees and foliage are worked in dark blue sprigged fabric and in different tones of brown plain and sprigged fabrics. The flower beds are made with hexagons in red, white and pale blue flowered fabrics. Flower motifs have been cut out and backed with iron-on interfacing to stiffen them, then sewn to the flower beds, with the petals left free of the background.

The hills behind the cottage are worked in cream and beige patterned hexagons, and the sky in blue-grey, with pale blue and pink and white hexagons for clouds.

## Appliqué and embroidery

The cottage shape is worked separately (Fig 1). The roof, windows, door and chimney are applied, then embroidery is worked to define details. Back stitch, Couching and Chain stitch can all be used to show the edges of shapes such as window panes and door panels. Running stitch worked across the roof from side to side suggests the slates, while fabric flowers, machine-satin stitched around their edges and cut out, are applied to the window box by working a cluster of French knots in the centre of each shape.

The garden path is appliquéd and outlined in black using stitches such as those used for the house details. Trees can be worked in Back stitch and Chain stitch. Finally, Running stitches add texture and interest to the sky, and tiny beads or French knots complete the wisps of smoke from the chimney.

## Quilting

Panels of this type of patchwork need to be quilted so that when they are hung there is a play of light on the different areas of the design. Both machine-stitched and hand-sewn quilting have been worked (see page 137 for technique).

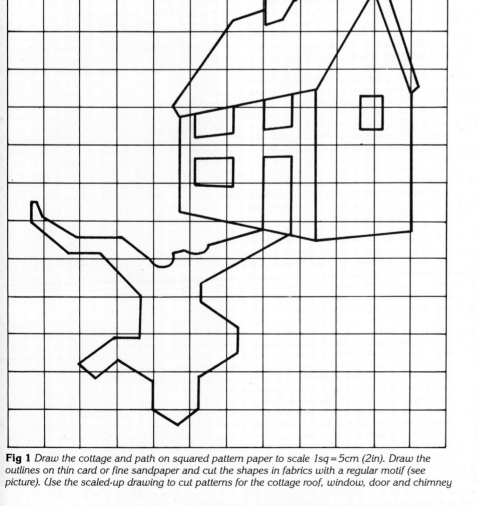

**Fig 1** *Draw the cottage and path on squared pattern paper to scale 1sq = 5cm (2in). Draw the outlines on thin card or fine sandpaper and cut the shapes in fabrics with a regular motif (see picture). Use the scaled-up drawing to cut patterns for the cottage roof, window, door and chimney*

# All about Patchwork

Patchwork has its beginnings in the need to make do and mend, but the fascination of modern patchwork lies in creating individual patterns and colour schemes using only the simplest sewing techniques. This chapter explains the basic equipment necessary and the first steps in patchwork.

## The history

It is almost certain that patchwork, which is acknowledged to have been in existence for over 3,000 years, started off in the poorer homes, where there was a very real need to make do and mend, and where no piece of fabric, however small, was thrown away. Only as late as the eighteenth century did patchwork join the crafts and skills of embroidery to become a leisure occupation for the ladies of the middle classes.

While patchwork is widely considered to be American in origin – indeed, it is almost possible to write a history of North America by making a study of its quilts – this is by no means so. The early English pioneers made extensive use of patchwork techniques from necessity because ships from home brought tools and seed, with little cargo space for non-essentials, such as fabrics and threads. The American people went on to develop their own special forms of patchwork, which today are referred to as 'piecing' or 'piecework'.

During the 1920s an archeological dig in the region of the River Ganges unearthed several pieces of patchwork which were estimated to date between the sixth and ninth century AD. They revealed some interesting facts, the most important being that in those days patchwork was made in exactly the same way as it is now, using the same stitch. One of the patchworks unearthed was made in silks, theoretically by a priest with pieces left for his use by travellers or pilgrims. The work is remarkable not only in colour and

design, but that it has survived in spite of being made of silk, a fabric that has notoriously poor lasting properties.

When, in the eighteenth century, patchwork became a recreation, velvets and silks were often mixed together. The velvets, being considerably heavier, pulled on the silks and destroyed them, so comparatively little work survives from this period.

## Making patchwork

Patchwork is an ideal way of making use of all those little pieces of fabric that have been hoarded away because they were far too pretty to throw out. You will probably find that you can make a whole bedspread without buying a single piece of fabric (except for the lining), and dressmaker friends will, undoubtedly, be pleased to help you with supplies of fabric. Alternatively, you can encourage them to join you and pool your resources. There is a lot to be said for this method of working when it is possible to share ideas, experiences and mistakes, as well as to gain inspiration from other people's work.

Once you have mastered the

*This double-size quilt was a group project and has been made with twenty 30cm (12in) blocks set around a central panel and borders. The blocks are based on a traditional American pattern – the Saw-toothed Star or Simple Star – which is a nine-patch block design. The central star is worked in appliqué. Triangles, squares and rhomboids make up the various areas of the quilt, and quilting has been worked to add interest and texture to the design*

# Patchwork templates

Here is the range of patchwork templates available in shops in pairs, a metal for cutting papers and a plastic window template for cutting fabrics. The arrows on the shapes illustrated indicate the direction of the straight grain of fabric when fabric patches are being cut.

**Hexagon** A six-sided shape with 120° angles. It can be used alone or with other shapes that have 120° or 60° angles.

**Rectangle** Half or one-third of a square, with 90° angles.

**Square** Can be divided into rectangles or triangles.

**Diamond** Also known as the Lozenge Diamond, with two 60° and two 120° angles.

**Long Diamond** A longer diamond shape than the lozenge, with two 45° and two 135° angles.

**Triangle** Three sides of equal length and 60° angles.

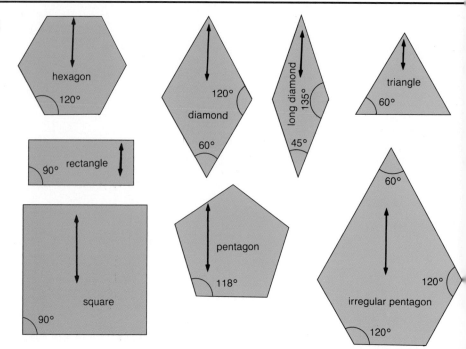

technique of applying fabric to paper you will find that the work progresses very fast. However, it is worth taking time initially to learn the correct technique, so that corners are firm and accurate. Nothing shouts quite so loudly as corners that do not quite meet, and no amount of beautiful stitching will cover up this fault.

It is a common fallacy to think that a first piece should be made with a large patch. For instance, a 10cm (4in) square will be more difficult to handle than a 2.5cm (1in) hexagon.

Skill in needlework is not one of the requirements for making patchwork, since one stitch only is used: a simple, small, oversewing stitch, which can quickly be mastered.

An eye for colour is a bonus in your favour. Many of you will have had some experience of achieving the right balance of colour in a room, and you will not necessarily have had a totally free hand – you may have had to work within certain colour limitations. So with patchwork: you may have a lot of fabrics but they may be of predominantly one colour. By purchasing a piece of fabric in a different or toning colour you will probably find that you can transform the rather ordinary item you intended to make into something very special.

# Materials and equipment

You will probably find that you have all the tools you need in your sewing box, with a few exceptions.

## Templates

Templates are the accurate patterns from which the fabric and paper are cut. (The fabric is mounted on the paper while it is worked into the design.) Most good craft shops sell various shapes of template, but if they are not available it is relatively easy to make your own out of good quality card, using a steel ruler, protractor, pair of compasses and a sharp crafts knife.

Templates are sold in packs of two. One is solid metal, which is used as a template for cutting out papers and is the size of the finished patch (Fig 1a). The second template is larger by 6mm (¼in) all round, to allow for seams (Fig 1b). The central part is clear plastic, so that when the template is placed over the piece of fabric the portion of a pattern that will appear on the finished patch can be clearly seen. By moving the template over the fabric you can find the area you want on your patch and centralise it (Fig 2).

In patchwork, when referring to a certain size patch, for instance, a

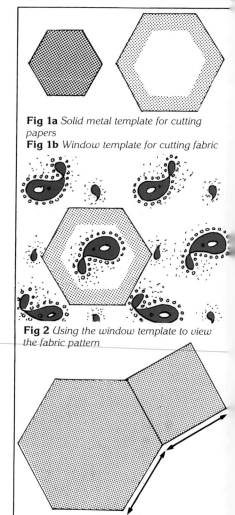

**Fig 1a** *Solid metal template for cutting papers*
**Fig 1b** *Window template for cutting fabric*

**Fig 2** *Using the window template to view the fabric pattern*

**Fig 3** *A 2.5cm (1in) hexagon fitted to a 2.5cm (1in) square*

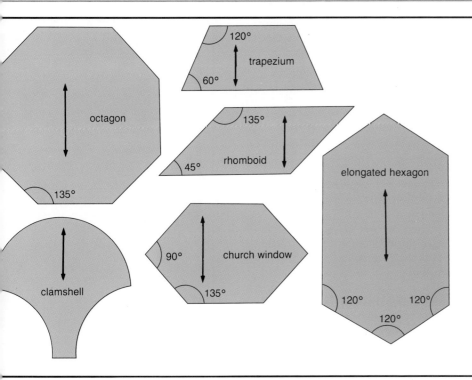

**Pentagon** A five-sided shape with 118° angles. It cannot be used alone to make patchwork.
**Irregular Pentagon** A diamond with a section 'trimmed' away, forming a shape with one 60° and four 120° angles.
**Octagon** An eight-sided shape with 135° angles. It must be worked with a square of the same size.
**Clamshell** This shape is always used alone but patterns can be built up with it.
**Trapezium** A half hexagon shape with two 120° and two 60° angles.
**Rhomboid** A shape formed with two irregular triangles, long edges making the sides of the rhomboid. The finer angle is 45° and the wider 135°.
**Church Window** Also called the Long Hexagon, with six equal sides, four angles of 135° and two of 90°.
**Elongated Hexagon** Also called the Coffin, with two sides of the same length and four sides of a different length. The angles are 120°.

2.5cm (1in) hexagon, this means that one side of the metal hexagon template has that measurement. Thus it is possible to mix a 2.5cm (1in) hexagon with a 2.5cm (1in) square (Fig 3).

## Scissors
You will need two pairs of scissors: one for cutting out the paper shapes (paper blunts scissors very quickly so keep them just for that purpose) and a sharp pair for cutting out the fabric. You may find a pair of small embroidery scissors is also useful, for snipping thread when sewing patches together.

## Thread
The traditionalists would observe the rule of using black or white cotton thread for all fabrics except silk, and silk thread in those two colours for dealing with all silks. Unless your stitching is near perfect it is preferable to use a selection of colours. Cotton thread, Nos. 50 or 60, is ideal unless you are working with silk fabric, when you should use silk thread. Synthetic thread is not advisable as you cannot work it into small, tight stitches.

## Needles
As you will be working very small, neat stitches, your needles should be fine: Nos. 9 or 10 'sharps' are best,

although many prefer to use what are known as 'betweens'. These needles are usually favoured by tailors and are readily available. They are much shorter and so do not bend as easily. However, with experience you will find out for yourself what suits you. You may find that the best method is to start with a large needle and progress to a shorter, finer needle as you become more confident.

## Thimble
Do try to become used to wearing a thimble. Without one you will find that, working with paper in your fabric, your middle finger will become punctured and very sore!

## Pins
Sharp, thin pins are essential. Buy glass-headed pins (made by manufacturers from discarded needles), which are excellent and easily seen when dropped.

## Paper
Good quality writing paper is used for making templates. Do not use shiny paper as the template will slip while you are working the patch. You should be able to feel the edge of the paper through the fabric when you are working the patch. Postcards are also suitable, but make sure that they are all of the same weight otherwise the size of your patches will vary.

## Other tools
As well as these basic tools, you may find it useful to have an unpicking tool, double-sided adhesive tape, beeswax for strengthening thread, a pair of compasses, a crafts knife and a steel ruler (which is easier to use with a crafts knife or wheel than a plastic one). Squared paper and isometric paper (ruled vertically and diagonally) are ideal for making designs, together with pencils and felt-tipped pens.

## Fabrics
Be selective with fabrics. Begin by sorting your hoard into fabrics of a similar weight and texture. Discard nylon fabrics and fabrics that will fray badly or are so thin that your turnings will be seen through the finished work. Discard, too, those fabrics with a high synthetic content: these are difficult to crease and to make into neat patches with good, flat corners and straight edges. Tightly woven dress cottons are ideal; so, too, are the semi-glazed cottons used for furnishings.

Mixing fabric textures and weights must come with practice. A patch made of cotton fabric will make a different finished size from one made of velvet. It is possible to compensate for the difference in weight by mounting the thinner fabric on to a bonding fabric and working the two as one, but this is more advanced work and should not be tried on a first piece.

Next, consider the item you would like to make. Bear in mind that if you are going to all the trouble of making, say, a quilt, you will want it to last for some time. If, on the other hand, you are making a fashion garment, you can disregard the fact that silky fabrics will not wear so well when used with tweeds and wools. Longevity will not be one of your considerations, rather colour, texture and overall eye-appeal.

## Basic techniques

### Making paper shapes

The basic geometric shapes used in patchwork – square, rectangle, hexagon, octagon and diamond – are, in essence, treated in the same way. The hexagon is used to demonstrate the basic techniques.

Cut out the papers, using the solid metal template, making sure the sides are straight and the corners accurate.

There are three ways of cutting the papers. You can hold the paper in

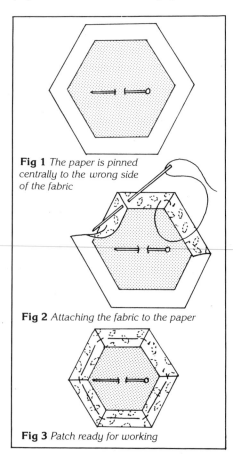

**Fig 1** *The paper is pinned centrally to the wrong side of the fabric*

**Fig 2** *Attaching the fabric to the paper*

**Fig 3** *Patch ready for working*

your hand, with the solid template held firmly over it, and cut round the shape with scissors, keeping the blades as straight as possible against the edges. You can cut several thicknesses at once but do not try to cut out too many in this way. It is difficult to maintain the correct angle with the scissors and you may find that the bottom papers are a different size from the top ones.

The second method is to draw round the template with a sharp pencil and then cut round the pencilled outline. If you are using this method take care to keep the pencil sharp and placed tight to the template.

The third method involves using a crafts knife. You will need a board on to which you can cut. Place your crafts knife next to the template on the paper and cut round. Alternatively, pencil the outline first, then cut out the shape with the knife, pressing against a steel ruler.

Whichever method you use, and all are equally successful, make sure the same method is used throughout the piece you are working, to avoid any variation in the finished size of the patches. It is a good idea to experiment with all the methods to find out which one suits you best.

### Mounting patches

Now choose the colours and patterns you want to work with from your collection of fabrics, and cut out several pieces, using the clear window template. Make sure that at least one side of the template is placed on the straight grain of fabric.

Take the first piece of fabric and pin a paper centrally to it, on the wrong side (Fig 1). With this in one hand and a threaded needle in the other, fold one side of fabric down over the paper so that you can feel a firm edge made by the paper through the fabric. Run your thumb and index finger across the edge to make a sharp fold. Turn the paper in your hand so that you can work the next side (Fig 2).

Having made your fold in the same way, insert your needle under the fabric just short of the pleat made at the junction of these two sides. Slide your needle under the fabric – but not through the paper – and bring it

## Flower pincushions

The pretty pincushions, looking like colourful flowers, would make an ideal first patchwork project. Each pincushion has only 14 patches so it is completed quite quickly and any scraps of fabric can be used. When finished, you will have a useful sewing accessory for your needlework basket.

Make two rosettes of hexagons using a 2.5cm *(1in)* template (see page

out on the other side of the fold. Do this fairly close to the cut edge of the fabric: if you stitch too close to the point of the corner, the stitch will not have enough retaining power and the paper will fall out. Take your needle back to where you first inserted it and make a second stitch over the first. The corner is now anchored.

Fold the fabric on the third side

132 for technique) and finish them as instructed on page 130. Pin the rosettes together, wrong sides facing. Oversew all round the 'petals', leaving the seam between two 'petals' open. Stuff firmly with polyester filling to make a rounded pincushion. Close the open seam with oversewing.

The round pincushion in the picture is an example of miniature patchwork and is made with 12mm (½in) hexagons. Both sides of the

pincushion are the same, made up with 13 hexagons in pale blue fabric (with 12 half hexagons set into the edges to form a circular shape) and six hexagons in a floral fabric. The pincushion has a 15mm (⅝in) gusset and is piped with the same pale blue fabric.

This hexagon design could also be worked as a full-size cushion. For a 25cm (10in) diameter cushion use 31mm (1¼in) hexagons.

making it easier to line up one corner with another when working them. It is, in fact, a great help to have an iron to hand at all times when working.

When working patchwork it is advisable to leave the papers in the fabric patches for as long as possible (quite a few will fall out with the handling of the piece of work), as they help to keep the shape and, particularly with a large piece, avoid unnecessary creasing. Do not reuse the papers: they will not have enough body second time around to give you an accurate shape.

## Cutting thread
Always cut your thread – breaking it also weakens it. Cotton thread is made up of tiny filaments spun together and there is a nap to it. For this reason, thread your needle with the end that comes off the reel first, and make a knot where you cut. Do not be tempted to thread your needle with too long a length of thread. The constant friction as it is worked through the material will also weaken it, causing it to snap. If you run the thread over a piece of beeswax, knots and tangles will be avoided and the thread strengthened.

## Planning colour schemes
When you have made several patches, lay them out on a flat surface and move them around until you are happy with the balance of colour and the mixture of plain and patterned fabrics. In this way, you will also be able to see whether you could add another colour to advantage or perhaps remove something. If you are working on a large project you may wish to pin each piece in place to a backing fabric – for instance, an old sheet – so that you can maintain your design in place over a period of time, removing each piece as it is required for sewing. For smaller projects you may find it helpful to pin patches to a soft board, such as a cork bathmat.

and work the corner in the same way as the first. Continue round the template until all corners are secured. It is not necessary to cut the thread between corners (Fig 3).

Remove the retaining pin and you should find that the paper is firmly lodged inside the fabric, even though you have not sewn through the paper. The advantage of this method

is that at the end of the work it is simple to remove the papers with thumb and forefinger.

## Finishing patches
You will find it an advantage to press the patches before you start sewing them together. In this way, the corners will lie flat and the angles formed by the corners will be sharp,

## Joining patches
You are now ready to start joining patches together. To do this small oversewing stitches are used, ideally about 16–20 stitches per 2.5cm (1in), picking up just a few threads of the

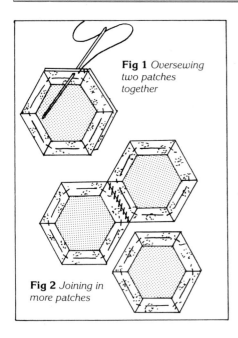

**Fig 1** *Oversewing two patches together*

**Fig 2** *Joining in more patches*

material but allowing the needle to glance over the edge of the paper.

Place two patches together, right sides facing (Fig 1). Start sewing about 1.5mm (1/16 in) in from one corner and work back towards the corner, sewing over the points twice to make sure they are firmly together. Now work across the complete side of these two patches till you reach the next corner. Oversew the corner twice and then work back 1.5mm (1/16 in). Make a double stitch and cut off the thread.

You are now ready to join in the next patch. Open and flatten the two joined patches and decide where the next patch is to be joined. Place the new patch on the chosen patch, right sides facing and aligning edges, and start sewing 1.5mm (1/16 in) from the corner as before. Continue in the same way, joining in patches (Fig 2).

### Finishing patchwork

Do not remove papers until all the patches have been joined. There is no need to remove the basting stitches. The stitches hold the raw edges of fabric down through wear and subsequent laundering.

You now have a piece of patchworked fabric and this is used to make items in exactly the same way as any other piece of fabric. If special techniques, such as lining or interlining the patchwork, are required, these are indicated in the project instructions.

# Basket of sachets

Lozenge diamond patches joined together into star shapes make pretty sachets. Filled with lavender and finished with a ribbon loop, they can be hung in cupboards to perfume clothes or linens. Line a basket with patchwork and fill it with sachets for a charming bedroom accessory.

### Basket

The basket measures 26 × 20cm (10¼ × 8in) and 43 hexagons worked with a 21mm (⅞in) template have been joined together to make the lining (Fig 1). There are 17 patches in plain pink fabric, 18 in white sprigged fabric and 8 in pink sprigged fabric.

Catch the edges of the finished patchwork to the inner rim of the basket and finish the edge with a strip of embroidered rosebud trim.

**Fig 1** *43 hexagons worked with a 21mm (⅞in) template, sewn together to make a lining for a 26 × 20cm (10¼ × 8in) basket*

### Sachets

Each sachet requires 18 lozenge diamonds worked with a 2.5cm (1in) template, six joined to make a star shape for the front, six for the back and six inserted into the angle between the star's points, joining front to back (Figs 2, 3, 4).

Leave one seam open, turn the sachet to the right side and pour in sweet, dried herbs or lavender through a paper funnel. Close the open seam with slipstitches.

Trim with a 30cm (12in) length of narrow satin ribbon folded as shown in the picture, and sew a single embroidered rosebud over the crossed ribbon ends.

If fine fabrics are used, the filling may show through. In this case, cut the fabric diamonds and then use the same template to cut diamonds from thin white fabric. Baste the two shapes together and mount on papers as one.

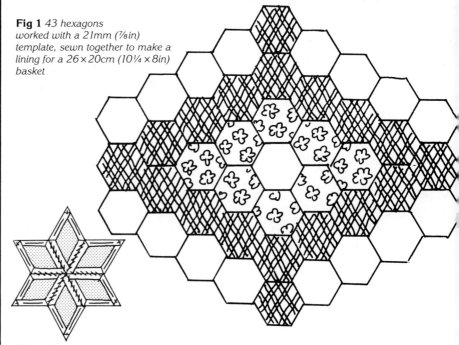

**Fig 2** *Six lozenge diamonds worked with a 2.5cm (1in) template, sewn together to make a star shape, from the wrong side of work*

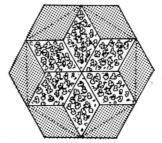

**Fig 3** *Diamonds are sewn into the angles between the star's points to join front to back. Fold the side patches on the dotted line*

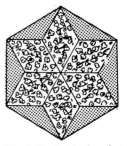

**Fig 4** *The finished sachet*

# HEXAGONS

The hexagon has six equal sides with 120° angles and can be used to form a number of patterns and designs without the need to introduce another patchwork shape. Hexagons are most associated with English patchwork and are the easiest shape to work with.

**Fig 1**

**Fig 2**

**Fig 1** *Six hexagons sewn around a seventh make a single rosette*

**Fig 2** *The addition of 12 patches makes a double rosette*

# Table mats

The table mats in the picture are made with 2.5cm *(1in)* hexagons. The techniques for mounting hexagon patches and joining them together are shown on pages 128–30.

Sew six hexagons around a seventh to make a rosette (Fig 1), then add another 12 hexagons to make a double rosette (Fig 2).

Finish the patchwork (see page 130), then, using it as a pattern, cut the same shape from plain lining fabric, adding 6mm *(¼in)* seam allowance all round. Turn in the seam allowance and oversew the lining to the wrong side of the patchwork.

## Designs with hexagons

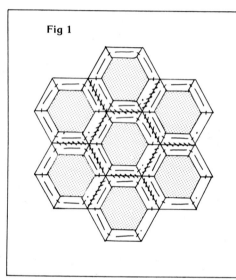

Hexagons are a favourite shape for making quilts, sometimes used in a pattern formation and sometimes at random. One of the most popular patterns is Grandmother's Flower Garden (Fig 1).

In this, rosettes are made with hexagons of flowered fabrics surrounding a central patch in a plain colour. The double rosette hexagons are traditionally cut from green fabric to represent foliage. These double

**Fig 1**

rosettes are then joined by white fabric hexagons to represent the paths between the flower beds.

This pretty pattern is sometimes adapted to other forms; the quilt on page 134, for instance, is made up of double rosettes adapted to elongated rosettes.

The Garland (Fig 2) makes an ideal border for a quilt, or it could be used to edge a skirt. If it is being used to edge a quilt worked with double rosettes, the Garland's rosettes could be increased to doubles.

Ocean Wave (Fig 3) is another possible edging pattern and is traditionally worked in toning colours, the palest on the inner row and the darkest on the outer.

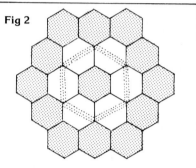

**Fig 2**

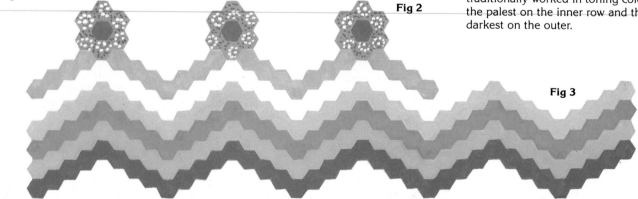

**Fig 3**

# Flower garden quilt

This modern hexagon-patch quilt is made with elongated rosettes (Fig 1), a variation on the way hexagons are usually used for quilts. Each rosette is made up of 25 hexagons and, like the traditional Grandmother's Flower Garden design, white patches are used to represent the paths between the flower beds.

**Fig 1** *Elongated rosette made up of 25 hexagons*

## Patches required

*Finished size 279×241cm (110×95in) including border*
Using a 2.5cm *(1in)* hexagon template: 2000 coloured patches; 880 white patches

## Working the design

Make up 68 elongated rosettes, each with a plain-coloured patch in the middle. Join white hexagons between rosettes when making up the quilt. Work half rosettes for the edges of the quilt and quarter rosettes for the corners (Fig 2).

## Finishing

The quilt in the picture is mounted on white fabric, turned on to the edges of the patchwork, making 10cm *(4in)* borders. The quilt has lines of quilting stitches along the 'paths' and through the patches of the rosettes (see page 136 for techniques).

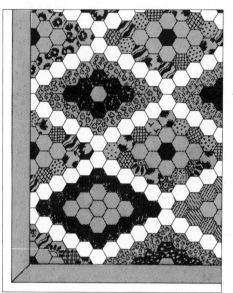

**Fig 2** *A corner of the quilt, showing half elongated rosettes at the edges and a quarter rosette at the corner*

*Right: Hand-sewn quilting has been worked through the centre line of the hexagons in a diamond pattern to secure the patchwork to its backing and give the quilt better handle*

---

# Estimating fabric quantities

Working out how much fabric is required for patchworks using diamonds or hexagons need not cause problems if you follow this method of calculating.

Having chosen the template — say it is a hexagon — first measure across the widest part of the window template (the one with which you cut fabric). A 2.5cm *(1in)* hexagon measures 6.5cm *(2½in)* between its widest points (Fig 1). From 91cm *(36in)*-wide fabric, therefore, 14 hexagons can be obtained from the width.

Now measure the template between the parallel sides — on the 2.5cm *(1in)* hexagon this measurement will be

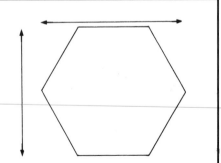

**Fig 1** *Measure the hexagon between its widest points, then between the parallel sides*

6cm *(2¼in)*. From a 91cm *(36in)* length of fabric, 15 hexagons can be cut from the depth. Thus, from a piece of fabric 91cm *(36in)* square, 210 2.5cm *(1in)* hexagons can be obtained.

# Finishing quilts

After the patchwork has been completed, quilts should be lined and the edges finished.

## Lining

For a double bed quilt it may be necessary to join pieces of lining fabric to achieve the desired width. It is preferable to join widths so that there is no seam down the middle of the quilt. Divide one width and seam the half-widths to the sides of the main piece. When lining very wide quilts, join as many pieces as required but always try to have a single width in the middle.

## Interlining

You may want to have an interlining between the patchwork and the lining, particularly if you are planning to quilt the patchwork. Interlining can simply be a pre-shrunk blanket, or use cotton or polyester wadding, which is available for this purpose.

## Attaching the lining

Spread the patchwork on the floor, wrong side up. Mark the middle of each of the four sides with pins. Mark the lining in the same way, then spread the lining on top of the patchwork, right side up. Pin the two layers together, first down the centre, smoothing the lining towards the edges as you pin. Then pin across from side to side, again smoothing the lining to the edges. If the quilt is very large you may need to pin in thirds or even quarters.

The easiest way to stitch the lining to the patchwork is to turn the edges of the patchwork to the wrong side and baste. Turn under the edges of the lining so that it falls short of the patchwork by a scant 3mm (⅛in). Hem the lining to the patchwork.

If a narrow edge of the lining is to show (such as on the Crazy Patchwork quilt on page 119), cut the lining 2.5–3cm (1–1¼in) larger all round and turn a hem on to the patchwork. Machine-stitch or hand-hem the edges.

Before the pins are removed the lining should be tied to the patchwork (see Working Quilt Ties).

## Borders

To work a fabric border, decide on the finished width and double this measurement, adding 2.5cm (1in). Measure the length and width of the quilt.

Cut and join strips so that you have sufficient for two long sides and two short sides plus 5cm (2in) on each length. Fold and press each strip lengthwise. Apply a strip along one side of the quilt, right sides facing and matching edges. Machine-stitch about 12mm (½in) from the edge (Fig 1). Fold the strip on its crease to the wrong side and hem to the lining. Apply the second strip, with the extra 2.5cm (1in) extending over the edge of the quilt. Machine-stitch as before (Fig 2). Fold the strip to the wrong side and hem, then tuck in the end of the strip, press and slipstitch neatly (Fig 3).

## Working quilt ties

Tying the lining to the patchwork is a time-consuming process but it is essential to prevent the ballooning that would otherwise occur.

The pins holding the patchwork to the lining should still be in position. Strengthen a long length of No.24 cotton thread by pulling it over beeswax. Thread a needle and, working from the lining side, take a 6mm (¼in) stitch through both thicknesses of fabric, leaving a 10cm (4in) end. Take another stitch in the same place and cut the thread with a 10cm (4in) end. Tie the two ends together securely. Cut off the excess thread, not too close to the knot. Work ties at 23cm (9in) intervals across and along the quilt.

**Fig 1**

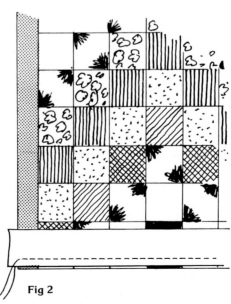

**Fig 2**

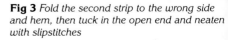

**Fig 3**

**Fig 1** *Apply the first strip to one side of the quilt, stitching about 12mm (½in) from the edge*

**Fig 2** *Fold the strip to the wrong side and hem. Then apply the second strip, overlapping the end and extending about 2.5cm (1in)*

**Fig 3** *Fold the second strip to the wrong side and hem, then tuck in the open end and neaten with slipstitches*

A very pretty effect can be achieved by using 1.5mm *(¹⁄₁₆in)*-wide satin ribbon for ties, finishing the double knot on the right side of the quilt.

## Quilting

A decorative effect (and better handle) is achieved by quilting. Traditionally, quilting is worked with running stitches but some patchworkers prefer to use a sewing-machine for speed.

To prepare the quilt, pin quilt, interlining and lining together, with the interlining sandwiched between wrong sides of quilt and lining. Baste the quilt from top to bottom, side to side and from corner to corner diagonally, through all thicknesses. Remove the pins.

Quilting designs can be impressed on the lining side of the quilt using a blunt-tipped needle, drawing the needle along a ruler or along the lines of a design drawn on tracing paper. Alternatively, use a 'pouncing' technique as follows. Pierce the lines of the tracing design with a pin, making holes about 3mm *(¹⁄₈in)* apart. Pin the tracing to the lining side of the quilt. Powder a little chalk or charcoal. Rub the powder along the holes so that a little goes through on to the fabric. Remove the tracing and draw over the line with a chalk pencil.

To work quilting properly, a quilting frame should be used because the stitch is made with a stabbing technique, passing the needle through with one hand and passing it back up through the quilt with the other. However, many quilters work without a frame and use a continuous running stitch.

Using No.50 cotton thread in a colour matching the patchwork as closely as possible, work neat, even-sized running stitches along the lines of the design, through all thicknesses of fabric. Thread ends should not be knotted. Begin and end with a double backstitch, leaving an end of thread. Re-thread the needle and draw the ends into the work.

The edging of the quilt is applied after quilting has been completed. There is no need to tie the quilt as quilting does the job of holding the patchwork to the lining.

## Miniature patchwork

If you like fine sewing and enjoy working in miniature, you can apply your expertise to patchwork. This beautiful, doll-sized quilt is worked with 12mm *(½in)* hexagons.

Great care has been given to the choice of floral fabrics for the central design, achieving the effect of a wreath of flowers. The flower heads are all of similar size and to scale. The design is 'lightened' at the edges by the use of pale-coloured patches with small sprig motifs in browns and reds, to give the impression of ferns and tiny leaves. The leafy effect has been emphasised by working quilt ties on the outer points of the hexagons, on the right side of the work. A group of four flowered patches is set at each corner of the quilt.

### Patches required

*Finished size approximately 38cm (15in) square*

Using a 12mm *(½in)* hexagon template: 343 cream patches; 125 patterned patches

### Working the design

Work a double rosette of cream hexagons for the centre of the quilt, then join four 'rows' of patterned hexagons round the rosette, using a sprigged fabric for the outer patches. Continue working with cream hexagons to the edges of the quilt, setting a group of four flowered patches at each corner, as shown in the picture.

### Finishing

Cut a piece of cream fabric 2.5cm *(1in)* larger all round than the finished patchwork. Press the patchwork with the papers in position, then remove the papers. Press the outer edges of the quilt again.

Turn and press a hem to the right side of the backing fabric, mitring the corners (see page 114). Baste the patchwork to the fabric on the edges and then machine-stitch all round, following the shape of the hexagons and working 3mm *(¹⁄₈in)* from the edges.

Work quilt ties on the points of the outer row of flowered hexagons and on the points of the four flowered hexagons at each corner of the quilt.

# SQUARES

Although squares are very adaptable shapes, they are not the easiest to work with because they must be accurately cut and joined. From the square, rectangles and triangles are obtained geometrically and thus a varied range of patterns is possible.

## Patterns with squares

Many of the traditional American block patchworks are based on squares, triangles and rectangles and by adding the diamond shape endless patterns are created. Blocks are divided geometrically, as shown in Fig 1.

### Joining squares

Squares can be joined by three methods. Machine-stitching, often used for making modern quilts, is quick and produces a strong finish. Hand-sewing, using small running stitches, is the traditional American technique. The third method is associated with English patchwork and uses paper templates (see pages 129–30). This method produces very accurate joins but is slow to work and is usually used only with small – 12–45mm (*1/2–1³/4in*) – square patches.

## Trip Round the World

This is a popular modern patchwork design and is made up of 5cm (*2in*) squares. In the quilt pictured, the arrangement of the patches leads the eye to see the squares as diamonds, and hand-quilting worked across the squares strengthens this impression. To vary the traditional design, rows of triangles have been worked around the central area of squares. The edges of the quilt are worked with Somerset patches (see page 140). The quilt measures 100cm (*40in*) square.

### Patches required

Using a 5cm (*2in*) square template: 21 red, 4 grey, 12 yellow, 20 pale pink, 28 turquoise, 60 mid-blue, 52 deep pink, 34 pale blue patches

Using a 5cm (*2in*) triangular template: 64 royal blue patches 5×9cm (*2 × 3½in*) rectangles for Somerset patches: 8 of each of the above colours

### Working the design

Join squares to make strips, then join strips in the sequence shown in the picture. Work triangles around the central area of squares and edge the quilt with Somerset patches.

### Somerset patchwork

Somerset patchwork is believed to have originated about 100 years ago in the English county of that name. The effect is of chevrons, formed by folding rectangles of fabric. The folded patches are worked on to a foundation fabric in rows or in rounds. See page 140 for the technique.

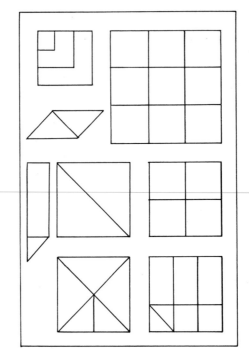

**Fig 1** *Squares can be divided geometrically to make smaller squares, rectangles and triangles, and from these, other shapes can be formed*

# Somerset patchwork

### Basic technique

1. Cut a rectangle of fabric on the straight grain 5×9cm *(2×3½in)*. Fold down a 6mm *(¼in)* turning on the top edge (Fig 1). Crease the fold with your thumb nail.

2. Bring the two top corners down to meet in the middle of the bottom edge (Fig 2). Press the patch lightly. To secure the patch, work two or three oversewing stitches 3mm *(⅛in)* from the bottom edge, through all thicknesses.

3. Arrange the patches in a row, with the points 12mm *(½in)* from the bottom edge, and stitch along the straight edges (Fig 3).

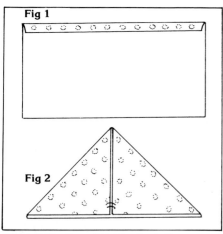

**Fig 1** *Fold a 6mm (¼in) turning to the wrong side on the top edge of the rectangle*

**Fig 2** *Bring the two top corners to the middle of the bottom edge. Oversew to secure*

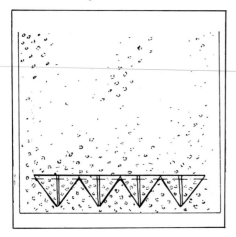

**Fig 3** *Arrange the patches in a row, 12mm (½in) from the bottom edge and stitch along the straight edges*

# Star banner

This striking banner illustrates the varied designs and patterns that are possible when working with squares, triangles and rhomboids. All the shapes in this patchwork are shown on page 138, Fig 1.

The banner is designed with 12 blocks joined with strips, and with small squares at the intersections. The two halves of the quilt, from the vertical centre, are mirror images. The fabrics, chosen from the Laura Ashley range, are co-ordinated in colour and pattern, and this adds to the overall harmony of the design.

Fig 1 shows the panel broken down into its 12 blocks. The panel, finished with quilted strips of patterned fabric at the sides, measures approximately 75×60cm (30×24in).

Additional interest is given to the panel with hand-quilting. A double-leaf motif has been worked in the central block, on the four squares and two of the triangles surrounding the eight-point star. More double-leaf quilting motifs link the half-blocks above and below the central block. Straight lines of quilting have been used to bisect squares, and the play of light on these quilted patches adds to the textural effect of the finished patchwork.

**Fig 1** *Diagram shows the banner's 12 blocks, made up of squares, triangles and rhomboids*

Fig 1

# STRIPS, RECTANGLES AND NON-GEOMETRIC SHAPES

Fabric cut into rectangles or long strips can be used to produce many different effects. Log Cabin, a popular strip patchwork, is worked around a square and is an appliqué technique. Somerset patchwork (see page 140), worked by folding rectangles, produces a three-dimensional effect. Strip patchwork is also a simple technique for making garments and fashion accessories. Cathedral Window patchwork is made by folding and refolding the fabric, and the finished results are very attractive indeed.

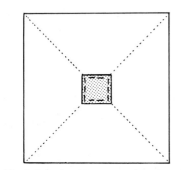

**Fig 1** *Sew the chimney patch in the middle of the foundation square*

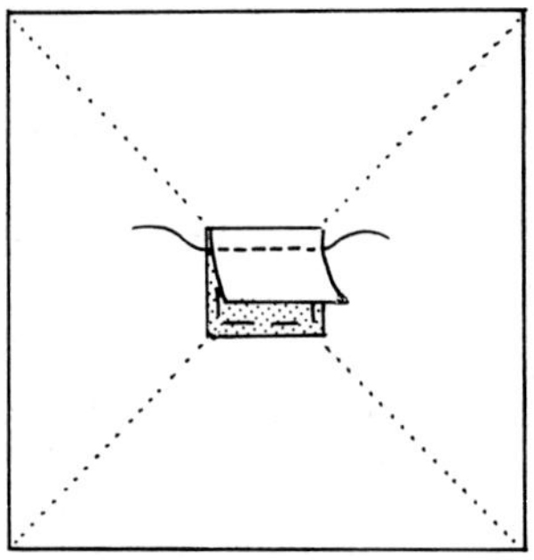

**Fig 2** *Lay the first dark strip on the square, matching raw edges, and sew in position*

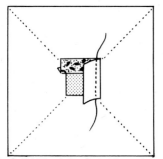

**Fig 3** *Fold back the first strip and sew the second dark strip in position*

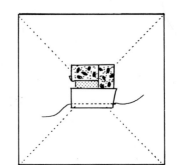

**Fig 4** *Fold back the second strip and sew the third, light-coloured strip in position*

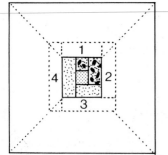

**Fig 5** *The first round of four strips stitched and folded back. The dotted lines show the order in which the second round of four strips is worked*

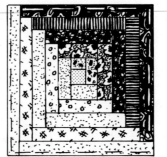

**Fig 6** *Five rounds of strips complete the log cabin block. Baste all round the edges*

# Log cabin

This is probably the best known of the old, American designs. As its name implies, the design is based on the traditional structure of a log cabin, the central square representing the chimney and the surrounding strips being the walls. One side of the block is worked in dark colours and the other side in light colours, depicting the firelight on the cabin walls and the shadows in the corners.

Log cabin can be made by hand or with machine-stitching and is worked on a foundation fabric in blocks. This means that fabrics of mixed weight can be used if desired.

**Basic technique**
Strips cut from light and dark fabrics are stitched in rows around the square

1. Cut the foundation fabric 30cm (*12in*) square. With a ruler, pencil lines diagonally from the corners to mark the middle. Cut the chimney patch 5cm (*2in*) square and place this in the middle of the foundation square. The corners should lie on the pencilled lines. Work running stitches all round the patch (Fig 1).
2. Cut strips from light and dark fabrics, across the width, and 4cm (*1½in*) wide – 2.5cm (*1in*) strips plus seam allowances of 6mm (*¼in*). Starting with a dark strip, lay it on the chimney square, raw edge to raw edge and right sides facing. Sew with small running stitches 6mm (*¼in*) from the edge, then cut away the strip level with the sides of the square (Fig 2).

3. Fold back the strip, away from the centre, and hold with pins. Turn the work. Using the same dark fabric, lay the second strip along the edge of the chimney square (see Fig 3, page 142). Position it from the corner of the square to the outer edge of the first strip. Sew, as before, with running stitches and cut off the strip. Remove the pins.

4. Fold back the second strip and hold with pins. Turn the work and, using the light-coloured fabric, lay the third strip along the square. Sew and trim as before, then fold the strip back (Fig 4).

5. Work the final strip of the first round in the same way and using the same light-coloured fabric (Fig 5).

6. Continue working round, keeping the light and dark strips to the same sides of the block as before, until you reach the edge of the foundation fabric (five rounds). Work basting stitches round the outside edge to hold the last four strips in place (Fig 6).

## Log cabin quilt

The quilt in the picture has 32 blocks, joined to make eight rows of four blocks. The border strips are 20cm *(8in)* wide. The quilt has been mounted on a backing 4cm *(1½in)* larger all round than the finished patchwork, the edges taken on to the right side and hemmed.

The quilt has been finished with quilting lines (see page 137 for technique), worked diagonally across the blocks.

# Shapes in harmony

The traditional Log Cabin pattern pictured on the opposite and previous pages inspired this wall panel but the techniques used in its construction are different. Nine blocks 20cm *(8in)* square make up the panel and each block is made by stitching strips of fabric into right angles around a corner square. The design has been planned so that attention is focussed on the apex of the panel, the darker tones being used in the lower blocks and the lighter towards the top corner.

To create movement in what might otherwise have been a rather static design, circles and arcs have been hand-quilted across the blocks. Instead of there being conflict between the two forms, a rhythmic harmony has been achieved.

## Wall panel

### Materials required

*Finished size 91cm (36in) square*
91cm *(36in)* square fabric for backing
4 strips 7.5×71cm *(3×28in)* for inner border
6cm *(2½in)* square fabric for each block
Strips for each block as follows:
Band 1: 1 strip 5×10cm *(2×4in)*;
   1 strip 5×6cm *(2×2½in)*
Band 2: 1 strip 5×14cm *(2×5½in)*;
   1 strip 5×10cm *(2×4in)*
Band 3: 1 strip 5×16cm *(2×6½in)*;
   1 strip 5×14cm *(2×5½in)*
Band 4: 1 strip 5×20cm *(2×8in)*;
   1 strip 5×16cm *(2×6½in)*

### Working the design

Fig 1 shows the arrangement of strips for each of the blocks. Taking 6mm *(¼in)* seams throughout, machine-stitch two Band 1 strips to the edges of a square, then stitch Band 2 strips to the edges of the Band 1 strips. Continue with Bands 3 and 4 to complete the block. Make nine blocks, then machine-stitch together in the arrangement shown in the picture. Join the inner border strips to the edges of the patchwork, overlapping the strip ends.

## Finishing

Lay the patchwork right side up on the backing fabric, centring it. Pin and then fold the edges of the backing on to the patchwork. Press the turnings under and hand-sew the edges of the backing to the edges of the patchwork, to make a border as shown in the picture.

The wall panel has been hand-quilted (see page 137 for technique) with circles over the corner squares and arcs across each block.

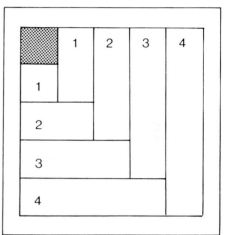

**Fig 1** *Each block is made up of eight strips of fabric stitched together to make right angles around a corner square*

## Strip patchwork cushion

The cushion in the picture is made in colours to tone with the wall panel. Strips are joined to make a 30cm *(12in)* square and two rows of Somerset patchwork (see page 140) add texture to the design. The finished size of the cushion, including the border, is 45cm *(18in)* square.

# Cathedral window

Cathedral window is a most effective form of patchwork, giving, as its name implies, the appearance of a stained glass window. The finished effect looks as though it is a difficult technique but, in fact, it is quite simple to work.

Cathedral window requires no lining and because each patch is applied to a foundation square and stitches are worked through all thicknesses, the whole piece is thereby quilted. The front of the work has the appearance of coloured windows and the reverse has a pretty, quilted effect. Cathedral window patchwork is therefore ideal for wall hangings or small quilts but probably looks best hung against the light, used as a window panel or blind as pictured.

## Fabrics

It is usual to choose a plain colour, such as white or cream, for the foundation as this contrasts well with the inset coloured or patterned patches and displays the subtle folds of the 'frames' to good effect. You may prefer to choose a patterned fabric for the foundation and a plain for the patches, but whichever scheme you decide on, use it throughout the piece. Mixed effects do not work well.

The foundation patches for cathedral window are 15cm (6in) squares of fabric folded down to 7cm (2¾in) squares. Quite a large quantity of fabric is therefore required for this type of patchwork.

Estimate fabric carefully and buy all you need at one time as plain colours can vary in tone and the variations will show in the finished piece.

A considerable amount of the work in cathedral window patchwork lies in folding and re-folding the fabric, so you need to choose a fabric

that takes creases easily. However, make sure it is a fabric that requires no ironing. Cathedral window patchwork should not be ironed after laundering as this crushes the folds.

The patterned inset patches are only 4.5cm (1¾in) square and, provided the fabrics are washable and colourfast, almost any small scrap can be used.

## Basic technique

1. Cut 15cm (6in) strips across the width of the plain fabric, on the exact grain of the fabric. Then cut the strips into 15cm (6in) squares, again making sure that you cut on the straight grain. The squares must be cut true to grain to ensure easy folding.
2. Cut 4.5cm (1¾in) squares from patterned fabric.
3. Press a 6mm (¼in) turning on all four sides of the plain squares (Fig 1). Fold each square and crease the fold lines with your thumb nail to mark the centre.
4. Fold the corners of the square to

**Fig 1** *Turn a 6mm (¼in) hem on all four sides of the square and press*

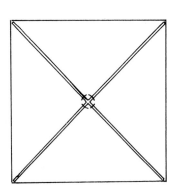

**Fig 2** *Fold the corners of the square to the centre and press. Backstitch all the corners*

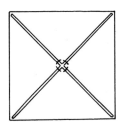

**Fig 3** *Fold the corners of the new square to the centre and backstitch*

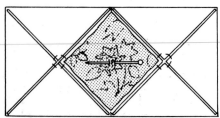

**Fig 4** *Pin a patterned patch in position*

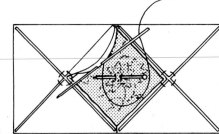

**Fig 5** *Roll the folded edge over the patch*

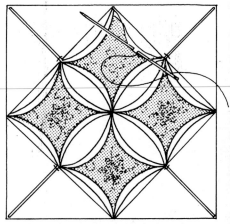

**Fig 6** *Work slipstitches along folded edge*

the centre and press the folds. Backstitch the four corners together in the centre and the four outer corners, to hold them in place (Fig 2).

5. Take the corners of this new square to the centre and press again. Backstitch the points together in the centre, first vertically, then horizontally, and taking the needle through all thicknesses of fabric. You have now completed one foundation square which should measure 7cm (2¾in) (Fig 3). Make several more foundation squares.

6. Using small oversewing stitches, join four squares, wrong sides facing, to make a block. Take particular care to match the corners.

7. Pin the first patterned patch over the seam between two joined squares (Fig 4).

8. Starting in the middle of the folded edge of the foundation square, where there is the maximum amount of 'give' in the fabric, roll – or draw – the edge over the patch for about 3mm (⅛in) and taper it off to a neat point at the ends (Fig 5).

9. Work a double backstitch at each point, across the two converging sides. Then work very fine slipstitches along the rolled edge through all thicknesses of fabric (Fig 6).

10. Continue joining squares and applying patches to them in the same way. Do not sew too many foundation squares together before applying the patches or you will have too much fabric in your hand to work comfortably.

## Cathedral window panel

The panel in the picture has 96 foundation squares, set 12 down and 8 across. A total of 2.85m (3¼yd) of 120cm (48in)-wide fabric is required for the squares.

There are 58 yellow patches, 28 green patches, 56 flowered patches and 30 sprigged patches.

On the outside edges of the panel, where there is insufficient space for a complete square, the folded edges of the foundation squares are drawn or rolled on to themselves and slipstitched in place.

# Chapter Twelve

# Machine Embroidery

If you can stitch in a straight line, you can do machine embroidery.
Simple patterns are possible using a straight stitch but a swing needle
can achieve more ambitious effects. Practise stitch and colour
combinations and brighten up a plain skirt hem.

You can use machine embroidery to make a variety of decorative effects on clothes, accessories and household linens. Striking patterns can be achieved using simple lines of straight and zigzag stitches and detailed pictorial and abstract designs are possible as you become more skilful at using the machine.

Freestyle machine embroidery is the most complicated technique and is worked without the presser foot and feed dog (metal teeth in the needle plate).

## What kind of machine?
Any sewing machine can be used for decorative stitching but, of course, the more basic the machine, the smaller the range of patterns which are possible.

**Straight stitch machines** By varying the length of the stitch and by moving the fabric in different directions, pivoting at corners with the needle in the fabric, you can create a limited range of simple stitch patterns. Leave the presser foot in the raised position when working in this way.

**Swing needle machines** By setting a short stitch length to make a close zigzag, and adjusting the stitch width, you can make wide or narrow bands of satin stitch. By lengthening the stitch but keeping a wide setting the zigzag elongates, reducing the density of thread on the surface of the fabric. Experiment with stitch lengths from the shortest to the longest that your machine can do. The closer the zigzag, the slower the fabric moves under the machine foot. Take care not to force the fabric through or you will get an uneven effect.

**A twin needle** can stitch many pretty double patterns using two different colours of thread for a variegated look. Remember not to set too long or wide a stitch – you could damage the needles if they strike the footplate.

**Embroidery stitch feature** Some of today's sophisticated electronic sewing machines offer up to thirty stitch patterns. Apart from the usual straight and zigzag stitches, they can sew scallops, triangles, leaves, feather stitch – even little trains for children's clothes.

Obviously your innovative abilities do not have to be so great – much of the credit for the decorative results will pass to the machine. There is, however, quite an art in choosing pattern and colour combinations.

In general, you need to decrease tension for decorative stitches of this

*Below: Plain and random thread machine patterns including a straight stitch pattern, satin stitch, a mirror image hearts border, a twin needle wavy line and a row of machine tailor's tacks*

kind to prevent the fabric from puckering. If it still puckers, try decreasing the tension on the upper thread even more.

## Fabrics and threads
As with all types of embroidery, it is a good idea to match the composition of thread to fabric – silk with silk, cotton with cotton and polyester thread with man-made fibres. All loose threads should be finished off at the back of the work or they may unravel during washing.

Adapt the thickness of the needle and thread to the weight of the fabric as you would for normal machine sewing. Light and open weave fabrics may be difficult to embroider without the fabric puckering. Tissue paper pinned

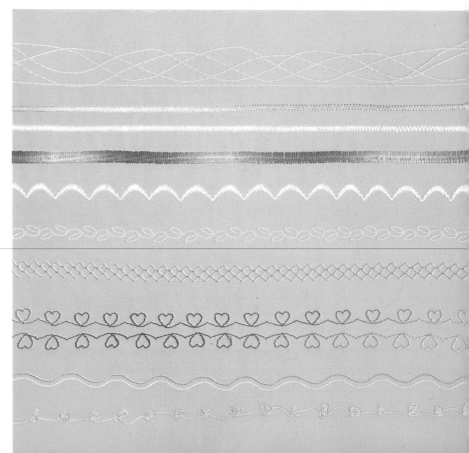

beneath the fabric helps – just tear it away after stitching. The more complicated the stitch, the more thread it will use – satin stitch, in particular, uses up a great deal of thread so make sure you have sufficient before you start.

Special cotton thread in a large range of colours is sold for machine embroidery, including some random dyed shades which gradually change colour, but ordinary cotton machine twist is perfectly suitable.

Embroidery threads such as pearl cotton look very pretty and give greater emphasis to the pattern as they are more loosely twisted than regular thread. Other alternatives are silk twist which comes in glowing shades, and metallic threads which are fun to use.

All these thicker threads must be wound on to the bobbin as they cannot be used as the top thread. Work the embroidery on the *wrong* side of the fabric so that the decorative thread appears on the right side.

You may need to alter the tension on the machine so that the lower, thicker thread is held in position by the upper thread and not pulled through the fabric.

## Patterns and stitches

Successful machine embroidery is the result of experimentation. Do try out the effects to see if the colours and stitches work well together and to check that the fabric is suitable. Consult your machine manual for any specific suggestions regarding needle size, tension adjustment, needle position, stitch length, and so on. Try as many different settings on your machine as possible.

Remember that simple embroidery can often be more effective than more complicated patterns so don't be too ambitious to start with.

## Machine embroidery tips

Before you start, clean the machine with a soft cloth to remove any excess oil and lint which could spoil your work.

Press the fabric to be embroidered so that it is completely smooth.

Mark stitching lines and patterns on the fabric with dressmaker's chalk pencil and brush it off afterwards.

After completing a line of stitching, leave an end on the right side long enough to be threaded through to the wrong side afterwards. When the embroidery is complete, knot all ends securely and trim off.

# Machine embroidery for a personal touch

Add a finishing touch to purchased items or things you have sewn yourself. The effect you achieve can be either subtle or bold. This is determined by your choice of colours and stitches.

Personalize anything from a plain hanky to collars, cuffs, pockets, sash belts, dress yokes, aprons, sheets, pillowcases and tablecloths. Little girls' plain skirts can be given a really festive

*Above: Design a set of linen table napkins with coloured lines and squiggles to match a tablecloth*

look with some bright machine embroidery.

Try geometric designs on tablecloths and napkins – use a zigzag satin stitch for this. Scatter the cloth with boxes, squiggles and triangles to match your other furnishings. Try out some of the random-dyed threads in pastel colours. These also look stunning on the yoke of a plain white cotton dress, or used in a pretty scallop trim for a baby's dress.

combination of machine embroidery and decorative ribbon

random dyed thread for dress

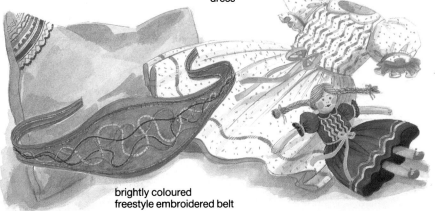

brightly coloured freestyle embroidered belt

# Machine embroidery on a skirt hem and matching shawl

A few rows of very basic machine embroidery have made the plain cotton dirndl skirt and shawl (shown opposite) into something special. By matching tops and accessories with the stitchery on the skirt, you can create a lovely co-ordinating outfit. Although a machine with embroidery features was used, most of the stitching was done with zigzag, using different stitch settings.

## The skirt hem

A plain white cotton skirt was chosen but the same colourful embroidery would look equally good on a black skirt.

### Materials required
Plain cotton skirt
3 reels of three different shades of cotton thread (this is sufficient for both skirt and shawl)
Dressmaker's chalk pencil

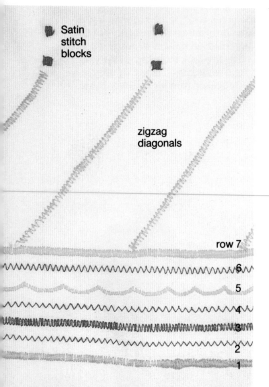

Satin stitch blocks

zigzag diagonals

row 7
6
5
4
3
2
1

### Preparation
The first band of embroidery lies 2.5cm (1in) from the lower edge of the skirt. Measuring carefully, mark this line at intervals with a dressmaker's chalk pencil. Practise on spare fabric to obtain a close satin stitch band.

### Working the embroidery
**Row 1** Beginning at one of the skirt seams, or one of the front edges if it is a button-through skirt, work close satin stitch all the way round to give a strong defined edge.
**Row 2** Mark a second chalk line, 6mm (1/4in) away from the edge of the satin stitch. Stitch along this row in your second colour, using the same width of stitch, but with a longer stitch setting to give a more open zigzag.
**Row 3** With the same colour in the needle, shorten the stitch length slightly to give an effect halfway between the first and second rows, and stitch a third row, again 6mm (1/4in) away from the second row.
**Row 4** Now repeat the stitch length of the second row, still keeping the second colour in the needle.

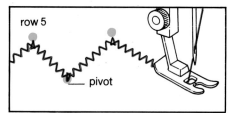

row 5

pivot

**Row 5** Change to your third colour to work a row of a decorative stitch such as the scallop used here. If you don't have a machine with an embroidery feature, try using a medium zigzag stitch to make a chevron pattern, pivoting the fabric at each point.
**Rows 6 and 7** Repeat the second row in the second colour before finishing off with another band of dense satin stitch in the third colour.
**Diagonals and blocks** The rest of the design is formed with a series of parallel diagonal lines in a medium zigzag stitch and each line is surmounted by two little satin stitch blocks. The 9cm (3½in) diagonal lines are 4cm (1½in) apart and slant at about 45°. Mark them on the skirt using a ruler and dressmaker's chalk. Practise working satin stitch blocks. Try to form neat 6mm (1/4in) squares about 6mm (1/4in) apart.

## Matching shawl

To complete the outfit make this easy shawl, it is simply made from a triangle of fabric.

### Materials required
1m (1⅛yd) of 112cm (44in) wide light cotton fabric to match or contrast with skirt
1 reel of three different shades of cotton thread

### Stitching the shawl
Trim the 112cm (44in) side of the piece of fabric to 100cm (40in) to make a square. Cut the fabric in half diagonally and tack a double 8mm (⅜in) hem along all three edges.

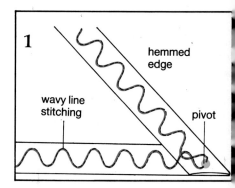

1
hemmed edge
wavy line stitching
pivot

1. Secure the hem with a row of decorative stitching, using a zigzag stitch variation or a wavy line.

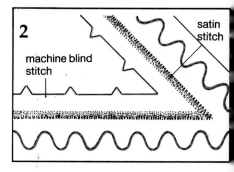

2
machine blind stitch
satin stitch

2. Follow this with another two rows, keeping 6mm (1/4in) between the rows as on the skirt. You can use satin stitch, and machine blind stitch as here, or any other you like. Be careful to pivot the fabric neatly at the corners of the shawl.

If you are enjoying your stitching, you can continue adding as many rows as you like. For an extra professional look, decorate the waistband of the skirt, echoing the design used round the shawl.

# CREATE A PICTURE USING A SEWING MACHINE

Machine embroidery can achieve very professional results using a swing needle machine which is capable of free stitching without the feed dog. Two stitch techniques and a glowing range of machine embroidery threads were used to work these charming duck pictures.

Use freestyle machine embroidery to achieve a pictorial effect which is more flexible and creative than the simple decorative stitches used on page 150. Instead of using the machine with the feed dog and presser foot in their normal positions, the feed dog must be lowered or covered and the presser foot removed so that the fabric can be moved freely in all directions. With the machine set to zigzag an all-over long and short stitch effect is produced.

## Preparing the machine

As with all machine embroidery, freestyle work uses up a lot of thread, so always begin with a full bobbin.

Lower the feed dog (or cover with the special plate provided) and remove the presser foot. Lower the presser foot lever before beginning to stitch to maintain the necessary tension. Set the top thread tension to low – usually 3 – but this can vary slightly with different models. It is important that the bobbin thread does not come up to the fabric surface while stitching. If it does, loosen the top tension a little more.

Set a short stitch length and the stitch width at No. 4 and thread up the machine. You can use any colour except black in the bobbin.

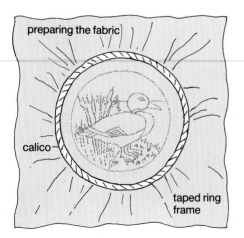

preparing the fabric

calico

taped ring frame

## Preparing the fabric

Firmly woven calico is one of the best fabrics to choose for machine embroidery. Mark the design on to the fabric, choosing a suitable transfer method (see page 9). Then mount the fabric in a ring frame, no larger than 20cm (8in) diameter. The small ring is on top of the fabric. To do this, lay fabric right side up over large ring, bind small ring with tape and push it in so that fabric is very taut. The fabric should lie absolutely flat on the footplate for stitching. Take care that the grain of the fabric is straight and the design is placed centrally in the frame.

## The stitches

Two basic stitching techniques are used to stitch pictures like the ones in these pages.

**Satin stitch** This can be made to resemble hand-worked satin stitch. The stitches should lie very close to each other and by going over the same row twice, you can produce a dense, raised effect.

Move the ring frame backwards or forwards as you stitch. The quicker you do this, the more widely spaced the stitches will be. Use this stitch to work solid blocks of colour or the more linear parts of the design.

**Darning stitch** To obtain a more random effect, move the ring frame from side to side at the same time as backwards or forwards. Quicker movements will produce wider stitches. Use this stitch for filling larger areas of the design with a textured look.

For both stitch effects, aim to keep the fabric moving continuously to avoid lumps of thread clogging the machine.

Remember to keep your fingers well away from the needle when stitching – it is not protected by the presser foot.

At stages throughout the embroidery, it is a good idea to remove the frame from the machine and tidy loose ends

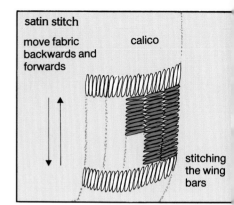

satin stitch

move fabric backwards and forwards

calico

stitching the wing bars

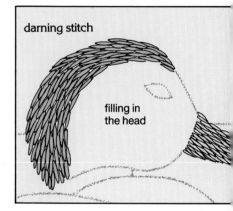

darning stitch

filling in the head

on both sides of the fabric by taking top threads through to the back with a crewel needle and tying each group of threads in a knot. Cut off the ends.

## Starting to machine

Thread up the machine with your chosen colour and bring the needle down into the fabric by moving the balance wheel towards you. Holding the top (needle) thread, stitch until the bobbin thread comes up to the top and pull through.

Start to machine steadily, following the lines of the design and moving the fabric in the frame by hand.

When you have finished a section, raise the needle from the fabric by moving the balance wheel away from you, and remove the embroidery. Cut both threads, leaving about 15cm (6in) to be finished off later.

Practise both satin stitch and darning stitch, moving the frame in all directions and experimenting with different effects until you can embroider confidently.

# Duck and drake machine-embroidered pictures

These charming pictures of a pair of mallard ducks set in landscapes each measure 15cm (6in) across. Special machine-embroidery thread in glowing colours has been used, including two random-dyed colours which give a lovely mottled effect to the sky and the ducks' wings. Work slowly and carefully, practising with each new colour to obtain the best effect for the area you are stitching. Try to consider the direction of the feathers and the way the

grass grows to achieve a realistic effect when stitching.

## Materials required
2 pieces of medium-weight unbleached calico, 30cm (12in) square
Orange dressmaker's carbon paper
Tracing paper
19cm (7½in) ring frame
Sewing machine needles No. 11 (90)
Crewel needle
DMC machine-embroidery thread Brillanté d'Alsace No. 30 in shades 5200, 783, 699, 796, 434, 898, 415, 105, 741, 93, 580, 711, 344, 644, 368, 437
Machine-embroidery thread No. 30 for bobbin (any colour except black)
DMC stranded cotton: 1 skein each of 989, 741, 367, 3371 and white
2 circles of stiff backing card (diameter of picture plus frame rebate)
2 × 16cm (6¼in) diameter frames with

*Above: If you have difficulty obtaining round frames or would prefer a square picture, either continue the landscape to fill the square area or have the circular embroidery framed in a square-edged mount.*

rebates (circular)
Buttonhole thread and needle for mounting and stretching work

## Preparation
Trace the main duck and drake outlines from the life-size photograph on to the tracing paper. Use dressmaker's carbon paper to transfer the design on to the fabric. Mount the marked area of the calico in the ring frame and work the stitching using the stitch guide and the colour key.

Work the stitchery in the order given in the stitch guide, the numbers refer to the parts of the design.

shade nos

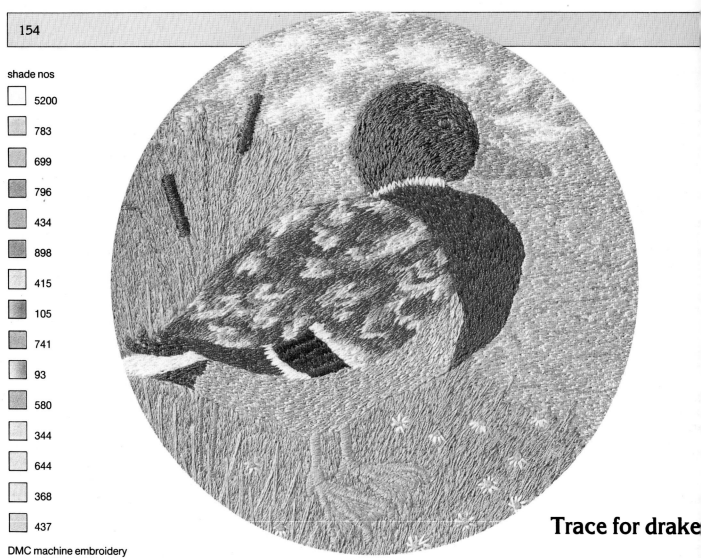

- 5200
- 783
- 699
- 796
- 434
- 898
- 415
- 105
- 741
- 93
- 580
- 344
- 644
- 368
- 437

DMC machine embroidery
thread Brillanté d'Alsace
No. 30 shade numbers

**Trace for drake**

# Working the drake

First, stitch the white collar from the back to the front of the neck – a single row of satin stitch.

Embroider the two white parts of the wing bar with close satin stitch.

Work the white tail with close darning stitch.

The drake's beak and eye area should be filled in next, using darning stitch.

Now fill in the green head area, following the contours of the head with darning stitch and blending the stitches into the white collar.

Add the blue wing bar using five rows of close satin stitch at right angles to the white feathers on the wing bar.

Use darning stitch to work the brown tail feathers above and below the white feathers. You may need to operate the machine manually to achieve the curves on the tail.

Embroider the chest area and the

bottom wing feathers below the blue and white bars in darning stitch.

The grey underpart is also worked in darning stitch, following contours as for the head and chest.

Change to the random-dyed thread to stitch the back and upper wing area with darning stitch. Guide the ring frame in a series of V-shapes so that your stitching looks like feathers. You may need to practise on a spare scrap of fabric.

Work the webbed areas of the feet in darning stitch and then the legs and toes in a close satin stitch. Taper the stitch width as you get towards the toes.

Now stitch the sky using the random-dyed blue thread and darning stitch with a horizontal movement. Do not forget to leave a space for the bulrush.

The lake is embroidered in two steps. First stitch some light blue reflections with a widely spaced darning stitch then set a close darning stitch and fill the remaining water area in grey.

The main area of grass is done with darning stitch. Turn the ring frame so that the drake is facing you and stitch with quick vertical movements so that the stitches are long and random, overlapping the sky and lake area.

Embroider the bulrush leaves in close darning stitch, the stalks in a row of vertical satin stitch (stitch width 1.5), and the seedheads with a vertical row of satin stitch (stitch width 4). Go over this row twice. Remove work from the machine.

**The hand embroidery** To add texture and depth to the picture, add a few simple stitches worked in two strands of stranded cotton thread.

The pupil of the drake's eye is worked as a double French knot. To work the reeds, make several long stitches, 1–2cm (½–¾in) in length. For daisies, make double French knots for the centres and tiny straight stitches for the petals.

## Working the duck

Stitch two white wing bars as for the drake, using two single rows of satin stitch. Add five rows of dark blue close satin stitch at right angles to the white feathers, between them.

Work the beak and eye as for the drake.

The head and chest dark areas are stitched next – fill in the dark area round the eye and small groups of darning stitch for the dark parts of the mottled head and chest. Continue with dark brown thread to embroider the dark areas of the wing, including a series of large V-shapes towards the back.

Now fill in the light areas of the head and chest, also the light areas of the wing. Alternate the V-shapes with the dark ones.

The whole of the back and tail are stitched with the random brown thread, again guiding the ring frame to simulate the features.

Fill in the webbed feet as before, then the legs and toes.

The sky is the same as for the first picture, as are the lake and grass. Remove embroidery from machine.
**The hand embroidery** Add reeds and daisies exactly as before. To stitch cow parsley, make one long green stitch for the stalk and five smaller ones at the top. With one strand of white thread, stitch French knots for the flower heads.

### Finishing

Remove each embroidery from the ring frame and press with a steam iron on the wrong side. Turn over and press under a damp cloth. Never iron directly on to the embroidery as this will make it shiny.
**Mounting and stretching** Mark a 28cm *(11in)* circle on the calico to give a 6.5cm *(2½in)* border round the embroidery. Cut away excess fabric.

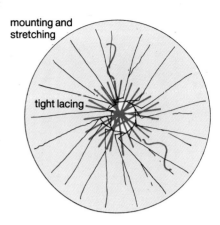

mounting and stretching

tight lacing

Place card circle on wrong side of embroidery. Thread a strong needle with buttonhole twist. Make a firm knot and take a small stitch about 1cm *(½in)* in from the edge of the calico. Lace tightly back and forth across the card, making tucks where necessary. Have the embroidery framed, or frame it yourself.

## Trace for duck

shade nos

| | |
|---|---|
| | 5200 |
| | 796 |
| | 898 |
| | 105 |
| | 741 |
| | 93 |
| | 344 |
| | 644 |
| | 368 |
| | 711 |

DMC machine embroidery thread Brillanté d'Alsace No. 30 shade numbers

# Place mats and napkins

White table linen gives an elegant touch to special occasions. In the picture, the linen has been embroidered in blue, the colour scheme taken from the china. Using a crisp piqué fabric with a squared pattern in the weave, it is a simple matter to follow the lines to work a machine-stitched decoration. Cream embroidery on white fabric would be a sophisticated variation.

## Materials required
*For six place mats 35 × 45cm (14 × 18in) and six napkins 45cm (18in) square*

2.40m *(2⅝yd)* of 120cm *(48in)*-wide white cotton piqué fabric
Sewing thread, white, light blue and dark blue

## Preparation
Press the creases from the fabric. Referring to Fig 1, measure and cut six rectangular place mats and six square napkins. Cut the mats 38 × 48cm *(15 × 19in)*. Cut the napkins 48cm *(19in)* square.

## Working the design
Set the sewing machine to a wide, close satin stitch. Following the picture, work two rows of dark blue satin stitching round each of the place mats, setting the outer row 5cm *(2in)* from the edge.

The napkins have a motif in one corner, consisting of two squares, one in light blue and the other in dark blue thread. Fig 2 shows the direction of the satin stitching. Use the squared weave of the fabric as a guide to working the embroidery. If desired, a square motif could also be worked in one corner of the place mats.

## Finishing
Fold and press a double 6mm *(¼in)* hem on all four sides of the place mats and napkins. Baste and machine-stitch, using white thread, stitching close to the edge. Mitre the corners, following Figs 3a, 3b and 3c.
Alternatively, a drawn thread edge could be worked for a pretty finish.

**Fig 1**

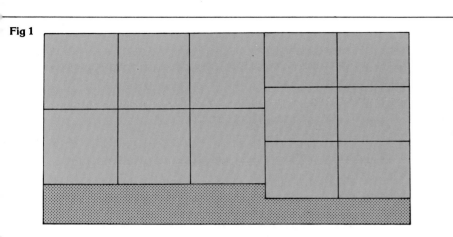

**Fig 1** *Fabric layout for cutting 6 placemats and 6 napkins from 2.40m (2⅝yd) of 120cm (48in)-wide fabric*

**Fig 2** *Work machine satin stitch along the squared weave lines of the fabric. Work the dark blue square first, then the light blue square*

**Fig 3** *Mitring square corners on linen: fold and press a narrow hem to the wrong side (A). Fold the corner on the inner, broken diagonal line and trim off the corner on the outer broken line. Press the turning (B). Fold the hems in so that the folded edges meet. Hem. Machine-stitch the hem (C)*

**Fig 2**

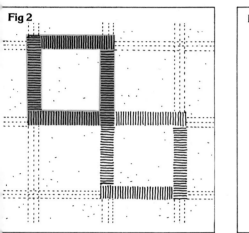

**Fig 3**

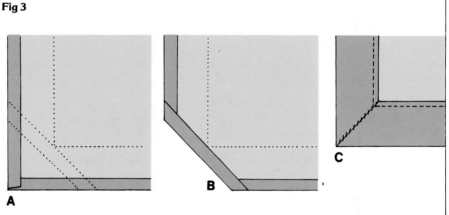

A  B  C

# Decorative napkins and place mats

Napkins and place mats made from plain fabrics can be decorated in different ways.
1  Stitch strips of washable, colourfast ribbons down one edge or across one corner.
2  Form ribbons into flower shapes and catch the petals and flower centres to the fabric.
3  Cut motifs from patterned fabrics and apply them to the napkin corners with close zigzag machine-stitching.
4  Print seasonal motifs, such as Christmas bells and holly leaves using cut potatoes and fabric paint.
5  Allow the children to draw motifs and faces on napkins and place mats then embroider the outlines with simple stitches such as Stem stitch and Chain stitch.
6  For special occasions, a striking table setting can be made by catch-stitching guipure lace motifs to the corners of dark-toned place mats. Add a smaller motif to the corners of napkins to match.

# Index of Stitches and Techniques

# Index of Projects

# Acknowledgements

The publishers acknowledge the help and co-operation of the
following designers and embroiderers:

  Jean Crowley (Crewel-work cushion, page 63)
  Beverley Jesset (Stitch samples, page 11; Cross stitch
    accessories, page 30)
  Josephine Kane (Arab shirt, page 21)
  Betty Laker (Gift cards, page 29)
  Vera Read (Long stitch picture, page 18)
  Lyke Thorpe (T-shirt, page 69)

Thanks also to the following companies and individuals who
helped with materials for this book:

  Sir Tatton Sykes, Sledmere, for the use of Sledmere's gardens and
    grounds

For permission to photograph their designs:
  Members of the London Quilters – Norah Field (Miniature
    Patchwork, page 137); Eve May (Crazy Quilt, page 119; Log
    Cabin Quilt, page 143); Jane Plowman (Friendship Quilt,
    page 120; Flower Garden Quilt, page 134)
  Jennifer Hollingdale (Trip Round the World Quilt, page 138; Log
    Cabin Quilt, page 144)

Child's lace dress on page 137 by Pat Smith, Hungerford,
  Berkshire
Dried flowers by Jane Thompson, Bromley, Kent
Berisfords for velvet and satin ribbons
Coats Domestic Marketing Division for threads and the place
  mat design, page 24
Dunlicraft Ltd for DMC threads and for their kind permission to
  reproduce the Cross stitch design charts on pages 32–3
Jem Patchwork Templates (distributed by Atlascraft), for
  supplying templates
John Lewis Partnership, London for lace trimmings
Madeira Threads (UK) Ltd for threads
NeedleArt House for Paterna Persian wools
C. M. Offray & Son Ltd for ribbons
E. W. Roper & Son Ltd, Nottingham for lace trimmings
Silvan Ltd, London for lace trimmings
Vilene Organisation for non-woven interfacings

All photography by Di Lewis, except the following:
  Eaglemoss Publications Limited – pp. 72, 106, 148, 149, 150,
    151, 153, 154, 155
  Coats Leisure Crafts Group – p. 72; Camera Press Ltd – p. 104;
  Pins and Needles Magazine – pp. 108–9; The Church of
    England Children's Society and Laura Ashley plc – pp. 122, 1[